UG, THE CAVEMAN MUSICAL

BOOK BY **JIM GEOGHAN**
MUSIC BY **RICK RHODES**
LYRICS BY **JIM GEOGHAN**
VIVIAN RHODES
RICK RHODES

★

★

DRAMATISTS
PLAY SERVICE
INC.

*Dedicated to the memory of Rick Rhodes
whose music continues to gladden hearts.*

UG, THE CAVEMAN MUSICAL had its world premiere at the San Jose Stage Company in San Jose, California, opening on June 2, 2004. It was directed by Rick Singleton; the music direction was by Nick Flynn; the choreography was by Dottie Lester; the set design was by Ching-Yi Wei; the costume design was by Paul Gallo; the lighting design was by Michael Walsh; the sound design was by Robert A. Havlice; and the stage manager was Marie Shell. The cast was as follows:

UG .... Jonathan Leavy
ARG .... Stephen Pawley
BOB/FATALATABA .... Timothy J. Meyers
TATATA .... Lianna Marie Dobbs
BANDALA .... Keite Davis
IG .... Shawn Platzker
OOLOOKI/NARRATOR .... Kevin Blackton

UG, THE CAVEMAN MUSICAL was subsequently produced by the Attic Theater Ensemble in Los Angeles, California, opening on January 19, 2007. It was directed by Jerry Kernion; the music direction was by Louis Durra; the choreography was by Terry J. Barto; the set design was by Jay Africa, Don Shirey and Jerry Kernion; the costume design was by Shana Targosz; the lighting design was by Matt Richter; the sound design was by Scott Charles; and the stage manager was Harold Wolf. The cast was as follows:

UG .... Danny Blaylock
ARG .... David Barnathan
TATATA .... Devin Sidell
BANDALA .... Michelle Maves
IG .... Derek Houck
BOB .... Kevin Fabian
OOLOOKI .... Thom Babbes
GRANDPA/FATALATABA .... Adam Tait
TA .... Emily Morris
OOO .... Becca Battoe

CHARACTERS

UG — The leader of a small group of cave people one million years ago. Handsome (for a caveman), brave, inventive, and somewhat childish.

BANDALA — Ug's woman. Pretty, faithful, sensitive, practical, and wise.

ARG — Another adult member of Ug's tribe. A few years older than Ug. Ug's best friend. Not as smart or good looking as Ug.

TATATA — Gorgeous. Knockout body. How did she wind up in this tribe! Cleaner and better groomed than the rest. Sexy and self-centered diva. Slightly younger than Bandala.

IG — A boy, a teenager. Wide-eyed, hopeful, enthusiastic, eager to learn.

BOB — Yes, there were cavemen named Bob. Animated, energetic, and fussy bordering on crabby. Short-tempered, sarcastic, and funny.

FATALATABA — Oolooki's right-hand man. A weasel, a mean, vicious little suck-up.

OOLOOKI — Snobby, arrogant, conceited, patronizing egomaniac. Also, voice of Narrator.

PLACE

A cave.

TIME

Long, long ago.

SONG LIST

ACT ONE

1. These are Incredible Times
2. The Cooking Song
3. She's Finally Out of Guys
4. Tingle
5. Where I've Never Gone Before
6. Famous
7. What Can You Do for Me
8. These are Incredible Times (playoff)

ACT TWO

9. Something We Call a Play
10. As If I Care
11. Now You Owe Me
12. King Neanderthal
13. The Cooking Song (reprise)
14. I'm a Boar
15. Where I've Never Gone Before (reprise)
16. Tingle (reprise)
17. These are Incredible Times (reprise)

UG, THE CAVEMAN MUSICAL

The setting is a cave long, long ago. As we begin, the stage is in complete darkness. Music up. In the darkness, we hear the voice of the Narrator boom.

NARRATOR. *(Offstage.)* In the dim, dark days of the distant past, a single cell began to evolve in the primordial ooze. And one day, emerging from its solitary existence, that single cell evolved into what we now call ... *(We see the faint outline of a solitary figure on stage. This figure is Ug.)* Man. The most intelligent living thing ever created. *(The lights come up to full. Ug, brave leader of his tribe, stands atop his favorite rock holding his favorite sharp stick.)*

UG. Look at the *body* on that chick! Mama! Yeah! *(Ug strikes exaggerated poses that display his bravery and greatness.)*

NARRATOR. The pinnacle of all that was. A creature far different from all other forms of life.

UG. You gonna finish that fruit?

NARRATOR. Man could not only stand upright and make tools, he could discover, he could explore, he could offer keen and farsighted opinions.

UG. I believe there are three kinds of people in this world: those who can count and those who cannot. *(The other members of Ug's tribe enter.)*

NARRATOR. And man learned important things. Eventually he was able to build civilizations. Civilizations that would provide him with many comforts ... cable television, subways where homeless people could live, and meat that comes in cans. But in the dawn of time, when man was just beginning, he struggled to survive and to make his life better.

SONG: INCREDIBLE TIMES

UG.
> WE USED TO HAVE NO CLOTHING AT ALL
> OUR LIPS WERE ALWAYS BLUE
> NOW WE KEEP WARM WITH TIGER FUR
> WHAT'S A CAT OR TWO?

OUR TRIBE IS LIVING LONGER NOW
GRANDPA IS TWENTY-NINE
UG and ARG.
  WE MAKE FIRE MOST EVERY NIGHT
  THESE ARE INCREDIBLE TIMES
ALL.
  THESE ARE INCREDIBLE TIMES
  WE LIVED IN TREES BUT THAT WAS TOO HIGH
  AND WE'RE NOT SWINGIN' ON VINES
  WE'RE STANDING TALL
  'CAUSE THESE ARE INCREDIBLE TIMES
UG.
  WE KNOW THAT DRINKING MUD'S NOT GOOD
  THAT EATING WOOD CAN MAKE YOU SICK
  AND WE ALL KNOW THAT YELLOW SNOW
  IS SOMETHING NOT TO LICK

  WE USED TO STAND IN THE RAIN
  AND PLOD THROUGH ALL THAT SLIME
UG and ARG.
  BUT WHEN IT'S COMFORT YOU CRAVE
  THERE'S NO BEATING A CAVE
  THESE ARE INCREDIBLE TIMES
ALL.
  THESE ARE INCREDIBLE TIMES
  WE LIVED IN TREES BUT THAT WAS TOO HIGH
  AND WE'RE NOT SWINGIN' ON VINES
  WE'RE STANDING TALL
  'CAUSE THESE ARE INCREDIBLE TIMES
UG.
  THE PAST IS GONE
  IT'S TIME TO MOVE ON
  AND LOOK INTO THE FUTURE
  WE'LL START WITH THE WHEEL
  IT'LL BE A BIG DEAL
  WE'RE GETTIN' SMARTER
  WE'RE GETTIN' STRONGER
  WE'RE GONNA STAY HERE
  A LITTLE LONGER

ALL.
 THESE ARE INCREDIBLE TIMES
 ALL YOU HAVE TO DO IS OPEN YOUR EYES AND
 SEE THAT EVERYTHING IS JUST FINE
 IT SEEMS LIKE HEAVEN
 'CAUSE THESE ARE INCREDIBLE …

 THESE ARE INCREDIBLE TIMES
 ALL YOU HAVE TO DO IS OPEN YOUR EYES AND
 SEE THAT EVERYTHING IS JUST FINE
 IT SEEMS LIKE HEAVEN
 IT SEEMS LIKE HEAVEN
 IT SEEMS LIKE HEAVEN
 'CAUSE THESE ARE INCREDIBLE TIMES

 INCREDIBLE TIMES!
(Song ends.)
UG. I'm hungry!
ARG. I'm starving!
TATATA. Famished!
BANDALA. Me, too!
IG. My stomach's talking to me!
ARG. When do we eat, Bob?
BOB. *(Annoyed.)* It'll be done when it's done! Now move away from the fire! Look at you! You're like a bunch of savages!
BANDALA. I wonder what Bob is making.
IG. I'm hoping it's dead horse the lions couldn't finish. *(The others agree, that's a tasty dish.)*
UG. Yum!
BANDALA. Slurp!
TATATA. Love that!
ARG. Drool!
TATATA. I like that too, but I'm hoping it's roast of porcupine.
UG. Ooo!
BANDALA. C'mon now.
TATATA. Love that!
IG. Tasty!
ARG. Porcupine is practical. You get a meal *and* you get something to pick your teeth with.

BANDALA. True.

IG. Comes in handy.

TATATA. Useful.

UG. Dental hygiene is important. *(Ug gets a basket and shows it to the others.)* And look at this, everyone. After we're done eating our burned meat, Arg and I have dessert.

ARG. We picked a basket full of sweet-juicy-red-things-that-won't-make-you-dead.

BANDALA. How do you know they're sweet-juicy-red-things-that-won't-make-you-dead?

UG. Huh?

TATATA. Maybe they're sweet-juicy-red-things-that-*will*-make-you-dead.

ARG. Oh for...!

UG. Women! Do you think we're stupid? We know these are sweet-juicy-red-things-that-won't-make-you-dead ...

ARG. Because we *tasted* them.

UG. And we're not dead!

UG and ARG. Duh!!!

OTHERS.

Ahhhh!   Smart move!   Never thought of that!

ARG. *(Sniffs.)* Mmm! Meat smells good when it's in a fire.

BANDALA. Tastes better, too.

TATATA. It has that smoky bouquet.

IG. Is it true you guys used to eat meat without fire?

TATATA. That was way back when.

BANDALA. In olden days.

BOB. Before you were born, kiddo.

BANDALA. Then we discovered fire.

UG. Hey, remember what we all said the first time we saw fire?

BOB. Sure do.

ALL. *(Scream.)* AAAAAHHHHH!!! *(They all chuckle.)*

TATATA. We were such hicks.

UG. I can't stand it anymore! I've got to know what's for dinner!

IG. Me, too!

BANDALA. I'm dying to know!

BOB. *(Exasperated.)* Don't your noses tell you anything? *(Sarcastic.)* It's so gratifying to cook all day and no one can tell what the hell it is! *(Ug and the others sniff.)*

UG. Could it be ...

IG. Don't tell me ...

BANDALA. It smells like ...

ALL. Boar!

BOB. You better believe it's boar! *(They all cheer.)*

ALL.

Mmm! All right! Pig meat! Good for you! *(Music up.)*

UG. I love boar!

TATATA. But cooking boar is complicated.

IG. Way complicated!

BANDALA. Boar is tough to make.

UG. I can never remember the recipe.

BOB. Oh, it's easy! Cooking boar is a snap.

SONG: COOKING SONG

BOB.

BOARS LIVE ALL ALONE
OR THEY LIVE IN A FLOCK
IF YOU WANT YOURSELF A FRESH BOAR
YOU GET YOURSELF A ROCK
YOU TAKE THE ROCK
AND HIT HIM ON THE HEAD
WHEN HE GETS A SLEEPY LOOK
YOU'LL KNOW THAT HE IS DEAD

UG. Dead's important?

BOB. Very important. If the boar's still alive when you cook him …

IG. Yeah?

BOB. Your gravy comes out all wrong.

ALL. Ah!

BOB. *(Sings.)*

THEN YOU GATHER SOME WOOD
AND THROW HIM IN THE FIRE
YOU CAN ADD SOME DIRT FOR FLAVORING
WHATEVER YOU DESIRE

COOK IT FOR HALF A DAY
POKE IT WITH A STICK
SERVE IT WHILE IT'S PIPING HOT
YOU KNOW YOU'VE DONE THE TRICK!

TATATA. You make it sound so easy.

BOB. It is.

BANDALA. Sounds easy.

UG. Until you try and follow all those directions. Fish!

IG. No one can remember the recipe for fish.

UG. Too complicated.

BOB. Aw, fish is easy! *(Sings.)*

    FISH LIVE ALL ALONE

    OR FISH LIVE IN A FLOCK

    IF YOU WANT YOURSELF A FRESH FISH

    YOU GET YOURSELF A ROCK

    THEN YOU TAKE THE ROCK

    AND HIT HIM ON THE HEAD

    WHEN HE GETS A SLEEPY LOOK

    YOU'LL KNOW THAT HE IS DEAD

ARG. How long does fish stay fresh?

BOB. Two, three hundred days.

ARG. Good!

BOB. *(Sings.)*

    THEN YOU RIP OFF HIS SCALES

    AND THROW HIM IN THE FIRE

    YOU CAN ADD SOME DIRT FOR FLAVORING

    WHATEVER YOU DESIRE

    COOK HIM FOR HALF A DAY

    POKE HIM WITH A STICK

    SERVE HIM WHILE IT'S PIPING HOT

    YOU KNOW YOU'VE DONE THE TRICK!

ALL. *(Bridge.)*

    THE SMOKE

    MIGHT MAKE YOU CHOKE

    AND LIONS AND GEESE

    ARE LOADED WITH GREASE

    AFTER THEY CROAK

    IT'S SOOTHIN'

    WHEN THE ANIMAL STOPS MOVIN'

    YOU'RE COOKIN' WITH WOOD

    YOU KNOW THAT IT'S GOOD

IG.

DINNER IS GROOVIN'!

GROOVIN'!

UG. That's a lot to remember. No one person can carry all that information in their head. Besides large animals are much more complicated.

BANDALA. Like deer.

TATATA. None of us know how to cook deer.

UG. Not like you, Bob.

BOB. Deer is very versatile. It's one of the few meats that's perfect for a formal dinner or a late night snack. I like to think of deer as "the other white meat."

BANDALA. But hard to cook.

TATATA. The recipe is impossible to remember.

BOB. Not at all! *(Sings.)*

DEER LIVE ALL ALONE

OR DEER LIVE IN A FLOCK

IF YOU WANT YOURSELF A FRESH DEER

YOU GET YOURSELF A ROCK

THEN YOU TAKE THE ROCK

AND HIT HIM ON THE HEAD

WHEN HE GETS A SLEEPY LOOK

YOU'LL KNOW THAT HE IS DEAD

IG. It takes days to catch a deer!

BOB. But think of the appetite you build up!

ALL. Ahh!

BOB. *(Sings.)*

THEN YOU GATHER SOME WOOD

AND THROW HIM IN THE FIRE

YOU CAN ADD SOME DIRT FOR FLAVORING

WHATEVER YOU DESIRE

COOK HIM FOR HALF A DAY

POKE HIM WITH A STICK

SERVE IT WHILE IT'S PIPING HOT

YOU KNOW YOU'VE DONE THE TRICK!

BANDALA. Bob, what about vegetables?

BOB. Try to avoid them. Not good for you.

ALL.

YOU KNOW YOU'VE DONE THE TRICK!

(Song ends.)

TATATA. I can't *wait* for dinner.

ARG. Me, too.

UG. Dinner's my favorite meal of the day.

IG. Dinner's our *only* meal of the day.

OTHERS.

That's true.   He's got a point.   Right.

(Bob appears with a small stack of wooden plates.)

BOB. I'm setting the floor. How many are we?

BANDALA. Um … it looks like we're ten for dinner.

BOB. Ten it is. *(Bob goes about setting the floor for dinner.)*

BANDALA. Only ten? How did we ever get down to ten?

ARG. How big was the tribe this time last year?

BANDALA. Fifty?

TATATA. Sixty?

UG. Seventy-two.

BANDALA. Ooo!

ARG. Are you sure?

UG. Of course. I kept count and scratched it on the wall. Two buffalo, three wolves and a duck … seventy-two.

TATATA. How did we lose so many people?

UG. I think it might have been the lions, wolves, snakes, tigers, brown bears, black bears, white bears, hippos, elephants, alligators, cougars, hyenas, leopards and people getting pissed off and killing each other.

OTHERS.

Right.   True.   I remember.

UG. Fire, floods, disease, locust, famine, drought, blizzards, fever, spiders, ice storms, mud slides and earthquakes.

OTHERS.

That, too.   I forgot.   Yeah.

UG. Poisons, falling trees, tar pits, sink holes, broken bones, deep snow, child birth and animal stampedes.

BOB. Last year sucked.

ARG. Two was a bad year.

BANDALA. And then there was those other tribes that kept attacking us.

ARG. *(Incredulous.)* Because their god is a loving and forgiving god but ours isn't!

IG. What was *that* all about!

BOB. That's *so* inconsistent!

BANDALA. So stupid!

UG. Jerks!

TATATA. Pointless!

BOB. Insane!

UG. Whatever the reason, we've lost a lot of people.

ARG. Don't get sad, Ug. When I think of all the people who have left us, you know, faces I'll never see again, I make myself feel better by telling myself the same thing.

UG. What's that?

ARG. "At least *I'm* not dead!" *(Arg, Tatata, and Ig drift away as Ug becomes lost in thought.)*

BANDALA. What's going on, Ug? I know that look.

UG. You now me so well. I've been thinking lately about life and living, and it seems to me we're here for such a short time.

BANDALA. So?

UG. So, why are we here? Have you ever asked yourself that? Are we supposed to do something? And if we are … are we doing it? After we're gone, will people remember us? Will people know we ever existed? I don't know. It seems lately I've had this ache in my belly that tells me no one will ever know I was here unless …

BANDALA. Unless what?

UG. Unless I leave something behind.

BANDALA. Ug, we're all leaving plenty behind.

UG. What do you mean?

BANDALA. Look at all the bones and pottery.

UG. No, it's … it's something more than that. I just don't know what it is. *(Bandala gives Ug a sympathetic look and joins the others. During the following, Ig and Arg bicker. Music up.)*

SONG: THE MEANING OF LIFE

UG.
> WHAT IS MY PURPOSE?
> IS THERE MORE THAN JUST THIS?
> WAS I PUT HERE ON EARTH TO FOLLOW A DREAM
> OR MERELY EXIST?
> I WOULDN'T MIND THE TEARS AND THE STRIFE
> IF ONLY I'D FIND THE MEANING OF LIFE

IG. Hey, Ug! Arg won't let me sit next to you!

ARG. I'm his best friend! I always sit next to him!

IG. Eat me!

ARG. Go die!

UG.

    DESTINED FOR GREATNESS

    OR TO WAIT OUT MY DAYS

    WAS I FATED TO LEAVE MY MARK ON THE EARTH

        IN MYSTERIOUS WAYS?

    WAS I MEANT TO GO SOLO

    OR ELSE FIND A WIFE

    WILL I EVER FIND

    THE MEANING OF LIFE?

IG. Hey, I always eat off that plate.

ARG. Not tonight, punk.

IG. Crap head.

UG.

    THE MOON IS MY ANCHOR

    THE STARS ARE MY GUIDE

    I FORGE AHEAD

    WITH MY EYES OPENED WIDE

    MISTAKES I HAVE MADE

    AND BRIDGES I'VE BURNED

    IT'S THE PRICE I HAVE PAID

    FOR THE LESSONS I'VE LEARNED

IG. That's my fur!

ARG. You mean it *was* your fur!

IG. I hate you!

UG.

    WILL MY NAME DISAPPEAR

    AFTER I'M GONE?

    WILL THE WONDERFUL THINGS THAT I CREATE LIVE ON AND ON?

IG. It doesn't even fit you!

UG.

    NOT KNOWING THE ANSWER

    CUTS LIKE A KNIFE

IG. You fat bastard!

UG.

    WHEN WILL I FIND THE MEANING OF LIFE?

IG. That's my knife!

ARG. It's mine now because I'm bigger than you!

IG. I've had it with you, Arg! Had it! Understand?

UG.

   WHAT IS MY PURPOSE?

   IS THERE MORE THAN JUST THIS?

ARG. Let go!

IG. Noooo!

UG.

   WAS I PUT HERE ON EARTH TO FOLLOW A DREAM

   OR MERELY EXIST?

IG. You greedy asshole!

UG.

   I WOULDN'T MIND THE TEARS AND THE STRIFE

IG. I'll wait until you're asleep …

UG.

   IF I ONLY FIND THE MEANING OF LIFE

IG. Then I'm gonna *kill* you!

UG.

   IF I ONLY FIND THE MEANING OF LIFE

(Song Ends. Tatata approaches Arg and she turns on the sexy charm.)

TATATA. Tasting the sweet juicy red things to make sure they won't make you dead … That was smart.

ARG. Well, it was Ug's idea. *(Proudly.)* But I did the tasting!

TATATA. They'll go good with boar. I love boar. Don't you, Arg?

ARG. Well, I uh, um …

TATATA. *(Giggles.)* You're so witty! When I eat boar, my fingers get greasy.

ARG. Uh-huh.

TATATA. My fingers get greasy, then I run them through my hair. My hair looks good with boar grease in it, don't you think?

ARG. Huh?

TATATA. *(Laughs.) Love* witty men! *(Then.)* And, if there's a lot of grease, I like to rub it on my skin. Boar grease makes my skin look … nice. Don't you think?

(Arg eyes Tatata up and down.)

ARG. Yeah, you got nice skin.

TATATA. Ooo, when you talk like that it makes me so hot.

ARG. Maybe you're standing too close to the fire.

TATATA. It's not the fire, silly. It's *you. (Tatata giggles, gives Arg a "sex kitten" look and saunters away as Arg melts. Ug and Bandala approach Arg.)*

BANDALA. Well, it looks like Tatata is finding you not disgusting any longer.

UG. I think she's getting ready to do the grunt-naked-nah-nah-big-tickle with you.

ARG. You think?

UG. Well, she is without a man now.

ARG. True. When did her man die again?

BANDALA. Yesterday.

ARG. Aha. Still, she might choose you, Ug. *(Ug goes to speak but Bandala barges in.)*

BANDALA. Ug's not interested in a woman like that.

UG. *(Meekly.)* Yeah, I'm not.

ARG. There's also Ig.

UG. But Ig is only nine. He won't be ready to mate until next year.

ARG. And there's Bob, but …

BANDALA. But what?

ARG. Well …

UG. Bob doesn't do the grunt-naked-nah-nah-big-tickle with women. Bob does the grunt-naked-nah-nah-big-tickle with other men.

BANDALA. Oh! *(Then.)* What's that like?

UG. It's a lot like what we do except there's less begging.

BANDALA. Ah!

ARG. Well, if Tatata would like to do the grunt-naked-nah-nah-big-tickle I think I'll do well. I've been practicing on trees for a long time.

UG. *(Uncomfortable.)* Yeah, we noticed. *(Music up.)*

ARG. This is great news. I might very well have a chance with Tatata.

UG. More than a chance.

BANDALA. Look around, Arg. There's no one left except you.

SONG: SHE'S FINALLY OUT OF GUYS

ARG.
 I THINK I'M REALLY LIKING MY CHANCES
 LOOKS LIKE I'M FINALLY WINNING THE PRIZE
 I MAY NOT BE A PRINCE
 BUT MY ODDS ARE BETTER SINCE
 SHE'S FINALLY OUT OF GUYS

 LAST YEAR WE HAD A TERRIBLE FAMINE
UG. I lost a lotta weight.
ARG.
 DISEASE SURE HAD US FALLING LIKE FLIES
 MEN NUMBERED FORTY-THREE
 BUT NOW SHE'S DOWN TO ME

18

SHE'S FINALLY OUT OF GUYS

I SO ADORED HER
BUT I BORED HER
SHE BRUSHED ME ASIDE
BUT NOW SHE'LL SQUEEZE ME
PLEASE ME
SINCE ALL THE OTHER MEN HAVE DIED

SHE'S REALLY PLUMP IN ALL THE RIGHT PLACES
BANDALA. Be gentle with her!
ARG.
   A NICE BIG BUTT AND CHUNKY WHITE THIGHS
   NOW I MIGHT TAKE A BATH
   BECAUSE I'VE DONE THE MATH
   SHE'S FINALLY OUT OF GUYS

THERE WAS A TIME WHEN
I COULD
NOT TURN HER HEAD
BUT NOW SHE'S LOOKIN'
WE'RE COOKIN' 'CAUSE
ALL THE OTHER MEN ARE DEAD

SHE DOESN'T REALLY HAVE A SELECTION
OF MEN WHO ARE BOTH HANDSOME AND WISE
OR MEN WITH LOTS OF HAIR
OR FURRY SKINS TO WEAR
SHE'S FINALLY …
(Spoken.) Face it! It's me or nothing!

I'M ON THE BRINK OF REALLY
HAVING SOME FUN
I'LL FINALLY GET HER
I DO BETTER
WHEN I'M RUNNING IN A FIELD OF ONE

THOSE MEN WERE NOTHING BUT COMPETITION
I'M GLAD THEY FINALLY SAID THEIR GOOD-BYES

I KNEW THINGS WOULD IMPROVE
I'M GOING TO MAKE MY MOVE
SHE'S FINALLY OUT OF GUYS
UG and BANDALA.
THINGS ARE IMPROVING
ARG.
SHE'S FINALLY OUT OF GUYS
UG and BANDALA.
'CAUSE YOU'RE STILL MOVING
ARG.
SHE'S FINALLY OUT OF GUYS

(Song ends. Bob burns his hand on the cooking fire.)

BOB. Ow! Shit! Damn! Shit! Shit shit shit shit shit shit shit! That's gonna scar. Shit shit shit shit shit! *(Matter-of-fact.)* Dinner's ready.

ARG. Okay!

TATATA. Let's eat! *(Arg and Tatata rush to the cooking fire, but Ig jumps in their way.)*

IG. Hold on. Not so fast. I think we should all wash to look our best when we sit down and feast on this boar.

ARG. What!

TATATA. Oh, come on!

IG. You guys are filthy.

ARG. We're always filthy!

BOB. I was born filthy!

IG. C'mon, you guys. You need to wash if you're going to feast on this wonderful boar! C'mon. Let's go. *(Ig ushers Arg, Tatata, and Bob out of the cave as they groan and complain.)*

BOB. I don't wanna wash …

TATATA. It's stupid …

ARG. What's wrong with being filthy?

IG. Come on. Come on. *(Ig exits after them. Ug and Bandala are alone now.)*

UG. *(Proudly.)* Ig is so young and yet he's telling the grown-ups what to do.

BANDALA. He's a natural leader. He's very much like you, his father.

UG. You think so?

BANDALA. That he's very much like you?

UG. No. Do you really think I'm his father?

BANDALA. I've thought about it a lot. Yes. Ig is probably your son.

UG. Good. *(They share a smile.)* You know, I've noticed something. When I think Ig is mine it makes me feel better somehow.

BANDALA. That's nice.

UG. And yet our tribe spends a lot of time guessing whose child was fathered by who.

BANDALA. It gets confusing, doesn't it.

UG. I was thinking, maybe we could end some of this guessing.

BANDALA. How would we do that?

UG. Well, when a couple joins together … you know they grunt-naked-nah-nah-big-tickle …

BANDALA. Yes?

UG. Maybe they should *stay* together. Then, when the woman has a child, there will be no arguing about who the father is.

BANDALA. Ahh! She's done the grunt-naked-nah-nah-big-tickle with only one man.

UG. And he's done the grunt-naked-nah-nah-big-tickle with only one woman.

BANDALA. That's very clever.

UG. Yes, it is. *(Music up.)*

BANDALA. But if you were to stay with me forever …

UG. Yes?

BANDALA. It would mean you have special feelings for me?

UG. I suppose I do.

BANDALA. What do you call these feelings?

UG. No idea.

SONG: TINGLE

UG.
CAN'T FIND THE WORDS
HARD TO EXPLAIN
BANDALA.
FEELINGS LIKE OURS
MUST HAVE A NAME
BOTH.
WE KISS AND I START TO HEAR THE RHYTHM OF MY HEART
I TINGLE, TINGLE, TINGLE
UG.
HOLDING YOU CLOSE
HERE IN THE DARK
BANDALA.
WHO KNEW A FLAME
COULD GROW FROM A SPARK

BOTH.
 I NEED YOU SO MUCH THAT I GO CRAZY WHEN WE TOUCH
 I TINGLE, TINGLE, TINGLE

 SECRETS TO SHARE
 A WORLD OF OUR OWN
 SO NICE TO KNOW

 THAT WE ARE NOT ALONE
 I'LL ALWAYS BE HERE
BANDALA.
 SENSING YOUR MOODS
 WILLING TO BEND
UG.
 I'LL BE YOUR ROCK
 I'LL BE YOUR FRIEND
BOTH.
 THE CLOSER WE'VE GROWN
 THE MORE I WANT YOU FOR MY OWN
 I TINGLE, TINGLE, TINGLE

 TINGLE, TINGLE, TINGLE
 TINGLE, TINGLE, TINGLE
(Song ends. Ug and Bandala are about to kiss. They are interrupted when Ig, Arg, Tatata, and Bob enter on the run.)
IG. Let's eat!
ARG. Gimme some pig!
TATATA. I want a piece that's low fat!
BOB. I want low carb! *(They all rush to the fire and grab pieces of boar. Bob holds off on eating, choosing instead to watch the others.)*
UG. Mmm!
BANDALA. Mmm!
UG. Mmm!
ARG. Mmm!
TATATA. Mmm!
IG. Mmm!
ARG. So good!
UG. Good boar, Bob.
BOB. *(Worried.)* Not greasy enough?

22

UG. No!

IG. Way greasy!

TATATA. So greasy!

ARG. Plenty greasy!

BANDALA. Extra greasy!

BOB. I dried it out.

UG. No!

IG. No way!

ARG. It's perfect!

BANDALA. Love it!

TATATA. It's *al dente!*

BOB. But it's overdone.

UG. No, it's not!

TATATA. It's greasy!

BANDALA. Lots of grease!

ARG. I'm swimmin' in grease!

IG. I'm chokin' on grease!

BOB. I should have made potatoes.

UG. Would you stop!

BANDALA. It's perfect!

ARG. Just the way it is!

BOB. Maybe a salad?

ARG. No!

UG. We like it!

BOB. *(Relieved.)* Good.

IG. Hey, Ug, remember the fierce, man-eating boar you faced a long time ago?

UG. How could I forget? I almost lost my life to that boar.

IG. Tell us how you killed him, Ug.

UG. Again? Aw!

TATATA. Yes, tell us.

UG. I tell that story every time we eat boar.

ARG. That's why we love hearing it.

BOB. The meal and the story all tie together. They dove-tail, so to speak.

UG. You want me to tell it again?

BANDALA. Yeah!

IG. We forgot how it goes.

BOB. We have very poor long-term memory.

BANDALA. Tell the story!

ARG. Please?

23

IG. C'mon, boar story!

TATATA. Yeah!

ARG. *(Chanting.)* Boar story! Boar story! *(The others join in.)*

OTHERS. Boar story! Boar story! Boar story! Boar story!

UG. Okay okay! Well, it was many rains and white seasons ago. The tribe was very hungry and I was ...

BANDALA. What's the matter, Ug?

UG. I don't know. I just wish there was some other way to tell this story. Make it more lively, more interesting.

IG. What could be more interesting than sitting on our asses listening to you talk?

BANDALA. Yeah.

ARG. He's right.

UG. *(Suddenly.)* Wait! I know! I know! Why don't I *show* all of you what it was like!

TATATA. How would you do that?

UG. By pretending!

OTHERS. Gasp!

TATATA. All of us?

ARG. Give up reality?

BANDALA. At the same time?

BOB. As a group?

UG. Yes! *(Ug jumps to his feet and grabs a sharp stick.)* I want all of you to pretend you were there.

ARG. What!

IG. There?

BOB. Not here?

BANDALA. You're not serious.

UG. I am. And pretend it isn't now. Pretend it is then.

BOB. Pretend *two* things?

UG. Yes.

BANDALA. At the same time?

UG. Yes!

ARG. That's dangerous.

BOB. We could explode!

UG. Nothing bad is going to happen. Trust me. Now watch ... *("Acting.")* It is many rains and white seasons ago.

TATATA. "Is?"

IG. He's using the present tense?

ARG. Shhh!

UG. The tribe is very hungry, and I am by the river seeking boar with my very

24

best sharp stick.

IG. Ooo!

BANDALA. I like this. I like it a lot.

BOB. It has immediacy.

TATATA. *(To Ig.)* Down in front! *(Music up.)*

SONG: (TO GO) WHERE I'VE NEVER GONE BEFORE

UG. Seek boar! Seek boar! Seek boar! I see the tracks of a boar!

OTHERS. Gasp!

UG. A large boar!

OTHERS. *(Louder.)* Gasp!

UG. A mean, fierce, ferocious, man-hurting boar!

OTHERS. *(Loudest.)* Gasp!

UG. I will follow the tracks as I seek boar! Seek boar! Seek boar!

BOB. I love this!

UG. *(Sings.)*
SOMETHING AMAZING
IS HAPPENING TO ME
THIS THING I AM DOING
IT TRULY SETS ME FREE
THE THRILL OF PERFORMING
IS ONE I CAN'T IGNORE
TO GO WHERE I'VE NEVER
NEVER GONE BEFORE

(Then.) I follow the tracks along the river. I come closer to the river. And closer to the river. And closer to the river. *(Ig takes his drink cup and splashes water on Ug. Ug, annoyed:)* I'm not *that* close to the river! *(Then.)* Seek boar! Seek boar! Seek boar! Where is boar? I see no boar. I must find boar.

ARG. *(Pointing.)* Stand over there, Ug.

UG. Over where?

ARG. Over there. Upcave.

UG. Upcave?

ARG. Yes, the floor slopes up so that would be upcave. We're sitting downcave. The fire shines more brightly there. We can see you better. And carry your sharp stick in your downcave hand. *(Ug holds the stick in the wrong hand.)* No, your *other* downcave hand. We can see it better. It will impress us more. It tells us right away we're into an "action slash adventure tale."

UG. *(Annoyed.)* Anything else?

ARG. Yes, as you seek the boar, try and look as if you are weak and hungry. It'll make us feel you stand little chance with this ferocious boar.

BOB. Those are good notes.

UG. Why don't you just do the story yourself?

ARG. If it's all right with you I'd rather step back, watch, and tell you how to do it.

UG. Oh!

ARG.

  AS TALENT SURROUNDS ME
  MY OPTIONS ASTOUND ME
  MOVING PEOPLE AROUND ME
  TO GO … WHERE THEY'VE NEVER GONE BEFORE

UG	ARG.
SOMETHING AMAZING	AS TALENT SURROUNDS ME
IS HAPPENING TO ME	MY OPTIONS ASTOUND ME
THIS THING I AM DOING	MOVING PEOPLE AROUND ME
IT TRULY SETS ME FREE	TO GO … WHERE THEY HAVE
THE THRILL OF PERFORMING	NEVER GONE BEFORE
IS ONE I CAN'T IGNORE	
TO GO WHERE I'VE NEVER	
NEVER GONE BEFORE	

UG. Okay … Let me start again. *("Acting.")* The tribe is hungry. I am weak. I am looking for food. Seek boar! Seek boar! Seek boar!

BANDALA. Hold on. *(Bandala grabs a boar skin and drapes it on top of her.)*

UG. Seek boar! Seek boar! Seek boar! Where is boar! I see no boar! The tribe will perish if I find no boar. Seek boar! Suddenly, look out, oh no, good golly, it's a wild, ferocious boar! *(Bandala jumps in front of Ug and gives a timid, little sound.)*

BANDALA. Arf!

UG. *(Appalled.)* Oh come on!

BANDALA. I do something wrong?

UG. *(To Arg.)* I can't work with people like this!

ARG. Can I talk to Bandala?

UG. *(Prima donna.)* Somebody do something! *(Arg takes Bandala aside.)*

ARG. Bandala, hon … Sweetie … Babe … Toots … What you did just didn't say "boar" to me.

BANDALA. It didn't?

ARG. Well, you tell me. Did it say boar to you?

BANDALA. I think I fell a little short.

ARG. You've got to reach inside, sweetie. All your pain, all your hurt, all your suffering, your guts, the guy you went out with before Ug …

BANDALA. *(Angry.)* That son of a bitch?!

ARG. Aha! Anger! Use it! It helps you find the boar that lives within you. You're not just playing a boar.

BANDALA. Uh-huh.

ARG. Girlfriend, you are a boar.

BANDALA. I am a boar?

ARG. You're a boar.

BANDALA. *(Stronger.)* I'm a boar.

ARG. I said you're a boar.

BANDALA. I'm a boar.

ARG. You're a what?

BANDALA. I'm a boar.

ARG. A what?

BANDALA. A boar!

ARG. A what?

BANDALA. I'm a God damn boar, asshole! Now get outta my way! Aaarrrggg!!!
(Singing.)
> DAG-GERS ARE WHAT I GET
> I'M LOOKED UPON BY OTHERS AS A THREAT
> WHEN THEY HEAR ME ROAR
> I'M FINALLY SOMEONE
> NOT JUST ANYONE

(Speaking.) Not some little person. Some little nothin'. Some insignificant piece of fluff no one pays attention to. I'm finally someone … *(Stops suddenly, then.)* Sorry … I'm dealing with some unresolved issues. *(Note: These three parts are sung together.)*

BANDALA.
> DAG-GERS ARE WHAT I GET
> I'M LOOKED UPON BY OTHERS AS A THREAT
> WHEN THEY HEAR ME ROAR
> I'LL SOAR … TO WHERE I'VE NEVER GONE BEFORE

UG	ARG.
SOMETHING AMAZING	AS TALENT SURROUNDS ME
IS HAPPENING TO ME	MY OPTIONS ASTOUND ME
THIS THING I AM DOING	MOVING PEOPLE AROUND ME
IT TRULY SETS ME FREE	TO GO … WHERE THEY HAVE
THE THRILL OF PERFORMING	NEVER GONE BEFORE
IS ONE I CAN'T IGNORE	
TO GO WHERE I'VE NEVER	
NEVER GONE BEFORE	

ARG. Okay, let's back it up to "suddenly boar." (*Ug goes back to his last position and runs through some familiar "actor warming up" exercises.*)

UG. Huba baka buba bubu! Ha babababa! (*Then.*) Ready. (*"Acting."*) Seek boar! Seek boar! Seek boar! Suddenly, look out, oh no, good golly! It's a wild, ferocious boar! (*Bandala leaps at Ug and lets out a frightening growl.*)

BANDALA. Aaarrrggg!!!

OTHERS. Gasp!!!

ARG. Loving it!

TATATA. I'm scared!

BOB. Too lifelike!

IG. Look out, Ug!

UG. Ug is trying to kill the boar but Ug is pushed against a large stone! (*Ug and Bandala reenact this.*)

BANDALA. Aaaarrrggg!!!

UG. The boar has very sharp teeth! Ug is cut! Ug is bleeding! Ug may die!

ARG. Don't die, Ug!

TATATA. Fight back!

BOB. Live, damn you! Live!

BANDALA. Aaarrrggg!!! Aaarrrggg!!!

ARG. This is working.

IG. I'm scared!

TATATA. Me, too!

BOB. This is so cool!

BANDALA. Aaarrrggg!!! Aaarrrggg!!!

BOB. Ug's gonna die!

TATATA. Don't die, Ug!

IG. Run, Ug!

ARG. Save yourself!

UG. Ug does not run! Ug is not afraid! Ug fights back with his very best sharp stick!

ALL.

   SUCH GENIUS AMONG US
   THE PRIDE THAT WE FEEL
   TO PLAY OUT A STORY
   AND MAKE IT SEEM REAL

   THE PASSION, THE DRAMA
   OF *UG AND THE BOAR*
   IS TAKING US SOMEWHERE, SOMEWHERE
   WE'VE NEVER BEEN BEFORE

(Ug pokes Bandala with his stick.)

UG. Ug fights! Ug is bleeding and weak, but Ug fights! Ug stabs the boar! Over and over! Take that, boar! Take that! Ug will not surrender! Ug left his tribe behind! They are hungry!

TATATA. He thought of us!

ARG. You're beautiful, Ug!

IG. I never knew that!

BOB. So butch!

UG. Ug stabs the boar over and over!

BANDALA. *(In "pain.")* Ew! Ew! Ew!

BOB. That is *so* S&M!

UG. Ug attacks! Ug fights! Then comes a moment. Ug looks into the eyes of the boar and let's him see the picture of his own death soon to come.

TATATA. Oh my!

IG. Awesome!

BOB. Beautiful!

ARG. I never expected this!

BOB. That's Ug, always throwin' you curves!

UG. Look, boar. Look into my eyes.

BANDALA. I see the land of death I will travel into. A land of all sunshine and no hunger.

UG. Give in to me and I shall put you there. *(Note: These three parts are sung together.)*

BANDALA.
   DAG-GERS ARE WHAT I GET
   I'M LOOKED UPON BY OTHERS AS A THREAT
   WHEN THEY HEAR … ME ROAR
   I'LL SOAR … TO WHERE, I'VE NEVER GONE BEFORE

UG	ARG.
SOMETHING AMAZING	AS TALENT SURROUNDS ME
IS HAPPENING TO ME	MY OPTIONS ASTOUND ME
THIS THING I AM DOING	MOVING PEOPLE AROUND ME
IT TRULY SETS ME FREE	TO GO … WHERE THEY HAVE
THE THRILL OF PERFORMING	NEVER GONE BEFORE
IS ONE I CAN'T IGNORE	
TO GO WHERE I'VE NEVER	
NEVER GONE BEFORE	

ALL.
   WHAT NEVER?

UG.

NO NEVER

ALL.

WHAT NEVER?

UG.

WELL, HARDLY EVER

ALL.

WHERE WE'VE NEVER GONE BEFORE!

OLE!

(Song ends. Arg, Ig, Tatata, and Bob cheer and applaud.)

ARG. Wonderful!

BOB. Fabulous!

IG. Incredible!

TATATA. That was like real life!

ARG. Like we were there!

TATATA. With you!

IG. And it was in *color!*

BOB. It was so graphic!

ARG. That changed my entire outlook on boars.

TATATA. I think I might only eat vegetables from now on.

IG. Me, too. Vegetables like wolf or eagle.

ARG. That was a wonderful story!

TATATA. So filled with emotions!

BANDALA. Danger!

IG. Excitement!

ARG. It was very now.

BOB. Very *mondo violente.*

BANDALA. I became the boar and felt its pain.

IG. I pretended I was you and felt your courage.

BOB. Ug, you've done it!

TATATA. You've invented a completely new way of telling stories!

IG. It'll change the future of story telling!

TATATA. Forever!

UG. You think?

ARG. Yes! Telling a story any other way from now on would be primitive!

BANDALA. Ancient!

TATATA. Obsolete!

BOB. This is the greatest invention *ever!*

IG. Boy, I'll betcha the Tall People got nothin' like it.

UG. What was that?

IG. The Tall People ... I'll betcha they got nothin' like it. *(Ug is thunderstruck.)*

UG. That's it!

BANDALA. What's it?

UG. My story. My story about me and the boar. Do you know what I'm thinking?

TATATA. What?

UG. I'm thinking about the Tall People and their visit to our cave next full moon. What if ...

BANDALA. Yeah?

UG. What if we show my boar story to the Tall People! *(The others react excitedly.)*

IG. Wow!

ARG. Yeah!

TATATA. Great idea!

BANDALA. Let's do it!

BOB. Love it!

IG. We'll knock their skins off!

UG. The Tall People are always showing off with things they've thought of.

BOB. Bragging assholes.

IG. Crap heads.

BANDALA. This will show them what a trendy tribe we are.

BOB. *Tres* trendy!

ARG. We're the cutting edge of the sharp stick.

UG. Yeah!

BANDALA. Modern!

ARG. Ug, if you're going to do your story for other people, you'll need to carry a bigger stick. It'll look more threatening.

UG. Fits my character! Yes!

BANDALA. I'll paint your face with ash so you look hungry and tired.

ARG. More jeopardy!

TATATA. You can never have too much jeopardy.

UG. Love it! *(Bob sizes up Bandala and measures her by eye.)*

BOB. And the boar skin ...

BANDALA. It was just something I threw on.

BOB. It needs ... hmm ... I'm not sure ...

ARG. I think it needs to drape on the side and ...

BOB. *(Snaps.)* Don't tell me what it needs!

ARG. Sorry ...

BOB. If anyone knows how a boar skin goes it's me!

ARG. Sorry.

BOB. Give me some time to think, will ya! I haven't put two thoughts together — you're already jumping down my throat!

ARG. I'm sorry!

BOB. *(Sweetly.)* I am, too. *(Then.)* Now then, boar skin, boar skin ... It needs to flow.

TATATA. Flowing would be nice.

BANDALA. And maybe some claws?

UG. Sharp, frightening claws!

BOB. Yes! I'm also thinking ... shhh ... don't rush me, don't rush me ... *tusks!*

OTHERS.

Ooo!   Yeah!   Wow!   Tusks!

ARG. The fire! We should have a very bright fire! A bright fire will cast giant shadows!

UG. So the story happens on two levels.

ARG. Exactly! Your story about you and the boar is downcave, real life, three dimensional, as it also dances on the walls upcave, larger than life in two dimensions!

BOB. I love it! I have no idea what you said but I love it!

BANDALA. Can we do it?

TATATA. I don't know!

IG. Do we have the time?

ARG. Do we have the *guts?*

UG. We'd have to put things aside, like searching for food and water.

TATATA. We could all starve.

BOB. We could get sick and die. *(Two seconds of silence. Suddenly:)*

ARG. Let's do it!

ALL.

Yeah!   All right!   Let's do it!   Okay!

TATATA. We'll get it done!

ARG. Yeah!

BANDALA. You know what, Ug. If the Tall People like your story, they'll speak of you everywhere they go.

ARG. She's right.

BANDALA. The Tall People are very well connected.

TATATA. Very plugged in.

BOB. They network with everyone.

ARG. You'll be famous, Ug.

UG. Famous? *(Pious.)* That's not why I create. Not for fame or glory or riches. I create to express my deepest, most intimate feelings. Still ... if fame should come ... *(Music up.)*

SONG: FAMOUS

UG.
  IT WOULD BE SO FABULOUS
  HOW LUCKY I WOULD BE
  FROM ORDINARY TRIBAL MAN
  TO BIG CELEBRITY

  I'M GONNA BE FAMOUS (YOU'LL BE FAMOUS)
  I'M GONNA BE FAMOUS (YOU'LL BE FAMOUS)
  I'M GONNA BE FAMOUS (YOU'LL BE FAMOUS)
  I'LL BE A HOUSEHOLD NAME

  THE PLACE I SLEEP AT NIGHT WILL BE
  THE CLOSEST TO THE FIRE
  THE THICKEST FUR, THE SHARPEST STICK
  WHATEVER I DESIRE

  I'M GONNA BE FAMOUS (YOU'LL BE FAMOUS)
  I'M GONNA BE FAMOUS (YOU'LL BE FAMOUS)
  I'M GONNA BE FAMOUS (YOU'LL BE FAMOUS)
  I'LL BE A HOUSEHOLD NAME

  I'LL ONLY EAT THE CHOICEST MEAT
  AS SOFT AS IT CAN BE
  AND IF IT'S TOUGH
  I'LL GET A FAN TO CHEW IT TWICE FOR ME

  FOLKS WILL COME FROM FAR AND WIDE
  TO SEE WHERE IT BEGAN
  AND WHEN THEY GET A GLIMPSE THEY'LL SAY
  "IT'S UG THAT FAMOUS MAN!"

OTHERS.

It's him!	It's Ug!	He's so cute!	What a doll!
Ug!	It's really him!	I'll have your children!	

UG.
  EVERYONE WILL COPY ME
  THEY'LL WANT TO HAVE MY STYLE
  I SING, I WRITE, I ACT, I DANCE

33

I'M VERY VERSATILE

I'M GONNA BE FAMOUS (YOU'LL BE FAMOUS)
I'M GONNA BE FAMOUS (YOU'LL BE FAMOUS)
I'M GONNA BE FAMOUS (YOU'LL BE FAMOUS)
I'LL BE A HOUSEHOLD NAME

FAME CAN REALLY CHANGE A MAN
IT MAKES HIS EGO FLY
I PROMISE THAT I'LL ALWAYS BE
AN ORDINARY GUY

I'M GONNA BE FAMOUS (YOU'LL BE FAMOUS)
I'M GONNA BE FAMOUS (YOU'LL BE FAMOUS)
I'M GONNA BE FAMOUS (YOU'LL BE FAMOUS)
I'LL BE A HOUSEHOLD NAME

I'M GONNA BE FAMOUS (YOU'LL BE FAMOUS)
I'M GONNA BE FAMOUS (YOU'LL BE FAMOUS)
I'M GONNA BE FAMOUS (YOU'LL BE FAMOUS)
I'LL BE A HOUSEHOLD NAME

I'M GONNA BE FAMOUS (YOU'LL BE FAMOUS)
I'M GONNA BE FAMOUS (YOU'LL BE FAMOUS)
I'M GONNA BE FAMOUS (YOU'LL BE FAMOUS)
I'LL BE A HOUSEHOLD NAME!

(Song ends.)

ARG. The Tall People are going to love it!

BANDALA. We'll wow 'em!

TATATA. This time, when they come for dinner, we'll have them eating out of our hands!

BOB. Actually, the last time they came for dinner ...

TATATA. Yeah?

BOB. They *did* eat out of our hands.

ARG. Oh, yeah.

BANDALA. That's right.

TATATA. They did.

UG. Sloppy. Arg, you'll help by telling us what to do, won't you? What looks right, what doesn't?

34

ARG. I dunno. If the Tall People like your story they'll throw fish heads.

UG. So?

ARG. So, if I'm working hard to make this happen, I should share in the wealth.

UG. Very well. You may have one fish head.

ARG. I want six.

OTHERS. Gasp!

UG. Six! Why you greedy, blood sucking bastard!

ARG. Hey, my ass is on the line, too!

UG. Listen, we asked for your help because we know you don't care about material things. You care about art. A single fish head, given to you from us, is our way of saying "thank you" to you, Arg. A man who shares our dream.

ARG. Six.

UG. Can't do more than two.

ARG. Six.

UG. Final offer ... three.

ARG. Six.

UG. We're done with four.

ARG. Six.

UG. Take it or leave it, five.

ARG. Six.

UG. Six.

ARG. Deal. *(Bandala cuddles up to Ug.)*

BANDALA. *(Sotto.)* Nice going!

UG. *(Sotto.)* I know.

ARG. We'll need lots of wood for the fire if it's going to be bright.

IG. I'll help.

BANDALA. Me, too.

ARG. You're not getting any of my fish heads! *(Bob, Ig, Arg, and Bandala begin to exit.)*

IG. Hey, Bandala ... if Ug becomes famous for playing himself, you'll become famous for playing the boar!

BANDALA. Yeah, guess so ... *(Roars.)* Aaarrrrgggg!!! *(Ig, Arg, Bob, and Bandala all laugh and exit. What Ig said has made an impression on Tatata. Ug and Tatata are alone now.)*

TATATA. Gee, Ug ... that's great. This whole thing that you invented. It's so great.

UG. Thank you.

TATATA. This new way of telling stories ... do you have a name for it?

UG. Gee, I dunno. I play myself ... Bandala plays a boar ... Play! I'll call it a play!

TATATA. Great name! I loved watching it. It was such a turn on. I mean it.

When I was watching I got so hot.

UG. You were sitting too close to the fire.

TATATA. No, I didn't get hot from the fire. I got hot from watching you tell your story, silly.

UG. Oh?

TATATA. And Bandala. She was very good.

UG. Yes, she has many features that remind you of a boar.

TATATA. And you're putting your future in her hands. That's nice. Take the gamble.

UG. Gamble? What gamble?

TATATA. Well … she could forget what sound a boar makes. Again. You'd have to stop your play. Again. Arg would help her. Again.

UG. No. She can't. We'll look like a bunch of amateurs! What would I do if that happens?

TATATA. I don't know. I guess you could find someone else to play the boar.

UG. Yes! But who else is there?

TATATA. Well, I might be talked into it.

UG. You? Aw, I dunno. Bandala lets me do the grunt-naked-nah-nah-big-tickle with her whenever I want. You and I, well we've never done the grunt-naked-nah-nah-big-tickle. Never.

TATATA. Well … maybe we can work something out … *(Music up.)*

SONG: WHAT CAN YOU DO FOR ME?

TATATA.
> I KNOW WHAT I CAN DO FOR YOU
> BUT I DON'T WORK FOR FREE
> I'D LIKE TO HELP YOU ALL I CAN
> TO BE A BETTER MAN
> BUT WHAT CAN YOU DO FOR ME?
>
> I'LL TREAT YOU GENTLE,
> I'LL TREAT YOU ROUGH
> I'LL DO IT TOTALLY
> AND WHEN YOU'VE FINALLY HAD ENOUGH
> I'LL ASK YOU WHAT CAN YOU DO FOR ME?
>
> I CAN WOO YOU AND DO YOU
> AND FLUTTER MY EYES

I CAN DANCE AND TWIRL AND
CRUSH A ROCK WITH MY THIGHS
I KNOW WHAT I CAN DO FOR YOU
BUT WHAT CAN YOU DO FOR ME?
(Sax solo.)
I CAN'T COOK OR SEW
OR WORK LIKE A SLAVE
MY TALENTS LIE IN ANOTHER PART OF THE CAVE
I KNOW WHAT I CAN DO FOR YOU
BUT BABY, WHAT CAN YOU DO FOR ME?

AS SURELY AS THE WORLD IS FLAT
I'LL BE THERE FAITHFULLY
I'D LIKE TO HELP YOU ALL I CAN TO BE A BETTER MAN
BUT WHAT CAN YOU DO FOR ME?
WHAT CAN YOU DO FOR ME?
(Tatata winds up in Ug's arms ready to be kissed.) So…?
UG. Okay! You got the part! *(They kiss. Song ends.)*

End of Act One

ACT TWO

A single spot shows on Ug's face. Music up.

SONG: SOMETHING WE CALL A PLAY

UG. *(Spoken softly.)*
   ON DARK NIGHTS
   WE USE BRIGHT LIGHTS
   ILLUMINATING OUR WAY
   IT'S ENLIGHTENING
   KNUCKLE WHITENING
   IT'S SOMETHING WE CALL A PLAY

   YOU GOTTA SEE IT
   TO BELIEVE IT
   IT'LL MELT YOUR TROUBLES AWAY
   IT'S ASTOUNDING
   ALL SURROUNDING
   IT'S SOMETHING WE CALL A PLAY
(The lights come up to full. Ug is joined by the rest of his tribe.)
ALL.
   ON DARK NIGHTS
   WE USE BRIGHT LIGHTS
   ILLUMINATING OUR WAY
   IT'S ENLIGHTENING
   KNUCKLE WHITENING
   IT'S SOMETHING WE CALL A PLAY

   YOU GOTTA SEE IT
   TO BELIEVE IT
   IT'LL MELT YOUR TROUBLES AWAY
   IT'S ASTOUNDING
   ALL SURROUNDING

IT'S SOMETHING WE CALL A PLAY

UG.

 I'LL SHOW THE WORLD
 HOW I FOUGHT THIS BOAR
 NEVER SHOWED ANY FEAR

GIRLS. What a man!

MEN.

 AFTERWARDS ALL THE GIRLS WILL SHOUT

GIRLS.

 "DID YOU SEE THE SIZE OF HIS SPEAR?"

UG. Hello!

ALL.

 FANS ARE FRANTIC
 YOU'RE GIGANTIC
 YOUR FAME AND FORTUNE WILL GROW
 YOU'RE A BIG SHOT
 NOW YOU'RE RED HOT
 YOU'VE GOT THE LEAD IN A SHOW

(As the music continues Ug performs a tap solo.)

ARG. What are you doing?

UG. This is my tap number.

ARG. I don't hear any tapping.

UG. It hasn't been invented yet!

ALL. Ah!

TATATA.

 ACTING ISN'T EASY
 IN FACT IT'S VERY COMPLEX
 IF THE AUDIENCE
 DOESN'T SEEM TO CARE
 YOU CAN ALWAYS GET 'EM WITH SEX

BANDALA. You would!

ALL.

 IT'S THRILLIN'
 TO CATCH A VILLAIN
 AS EVERYONE SHOUTS "HURRAY"
 FROM A ZERO
 YOU'RE A HERO
 IT'S SOMETHING WE CALL A PLAY

UG.

  DIM THE LIGHTING
  UP THE MUSIC
  WE DO IT ALL FOR A CAUSE
  THE JOY OF THEATRE, THE LOVE OF ART
  THE THUNDEROUS SOUND OF APPLAUSE
ALL.

  MAKE IT SAPPY
  MAKE IT HAPPY
  MAKE IT FUNNY
  EXCITING AND MORE
MEN.

  LEAVE 'EM CRYING
WOMEN.

  LEAVE 'EM SIGHING
ALL.

  LEAVE 'EM STANDING, DEMANDING "ENCORE"!
BOB.

  OUR NOTION
  TO SHOW EMOTION
  IS NOW BECOMING THE RAGE
  BE STUPENDOUS
  AND TREMENDOUS
  THE WORLD IS YOURS ON A STAGE
ALL.

  KNEES ARE SHAKIN'
  AND HEARTS ARE QUAKIN'
  OPENING NIGHT HAS ARRIVED
  THERE'S NOTHING QUITE LIKE
  THE THEATER LIFE
  TO MAKE YOUR DREAMS COME ALIVE
ALL.

  BE DRAMATIC
  CHARISMATIC
  SHOW YOUR STYLE
  AND THEN SHOW YOUR GRACE
UG.

  IF YOU DON'T GET A YAK
  FROM A JOKE THAT'S CRACKED

THERE'S ALWAYS A ROCK IN THE FACE
(Sound: Thunk!)
ALL.
    WHETHER SMASH OR DUD
    THEATRE GETS IN YOUR BLOOD
    AND YOU KNOW YOU'RE IN IT TO STAY NO OTHER ART
    GETS YOU HOOKED FROM THE START
    LETS YOU BE SOMEONE ELSE FOR A DAY
(Music stops.)
BOB. Mama! I'm in a new musical! I play a caveman! *(Music resumes.)*
MEN.
    LIKE SOMETHING
    SOMETHING WE CALL A …
WOMEN.
    SOMETHING, SOMETHING WE CALL A …
ALL.
    SOMETHING WE CALL A PLAY!
(Song ends. Ug and his tribe prepare for another rehearsal. Ig approaches Ug with a piece of tree bark.)
IG. Hey Ug, when the Tall People get here, I thought we could give them something to read while they're waiting for the play to start. *(Ug takes the bark from Ig.)*
UG. *(Reading.)* Ug and the Boar written by Ug. *(Then.)* Aha! A little background information!
IG. Yes! And I put everyone's credits on the other side.
UG. *(Reading.)* "Ug has never done anything. Tatata has never done anything. Arg has never done anything. Bob has never done anything."
ARG. What do you think?
UG. I love it! Make a couple more but make sure my name is bigger than theirs.
IG. Okay! *(Ig takes the bark and runs off to make changes. Tatata enters from outside.)*
UG. You're late! Where were you?
TATATA. Fixing my costume.
UG. What was wrong with it?
TATATA. It wasn't dead.
UG. Oh.
TATATA. Wanna see what I'm going to wear in the play, Uggy?
UG. That's not important! People won't come to plays to see costumes! They'll come to hear the *words* that the writer has carefully … *(Tatata holds up a skimpy, fur bikini. It stops Ug in his tracks.)* Hamina hamina hamina …
TATATA. Is it too skimpy?

UG. No, I like it, very much, very pretty, it's perfect. *(Bob approaches.)*

BOB. What's perfect?

TATATA. My new costume.

BOB. What happened to the one I designed for you?

TATATA. *(Cautiously.)* Well, I decided to go another way with it. What do you think?

BOB. I think you're insane! We open tomorrow night and you want to change your costume? Now?

TATATA. Can you finish it for me?

BOB. No way!

TATATA. Please?

BOB. You're out of your mind!

TATATA. Please, Bobby?

BOB. Can't be done!

TATATA. Please please please please please?

BOB. I'm not a wizard!

TATATA. Bobby …

BOB. There's not enough time!

TATATA. You're a genius.

BOB. Okay. *(Bob takes the skimpy furs and crosses to his work area.)*

UG. Ready to rehearse?

TATATA. Uh-huh.

UG. Okay, people … places … places everyone … We're going to take it from the top.

ARG. If you don't mind, that's *my* job.

UG. Sorry. Go ahead.

ARG. Okay, people … places … places everyone … We're going to take it from the top.

BANDALA. The top of what?

ARG. The top of the rock!

BANDALA. Ah! *(Everyone scurries to get ready.)* Very good. Okay then. Ready? And … action!

UG. *("Acting.")* It is many rains and white seasons ago. The tribe is very hungry, and I am seeking boar with my … *(Tatata jumps in front of Ug and growls.)*

TATATA. Arrrgggh!

UG. No! Not yet!

TATATA. Too soon?

UG. I have more words to say. Your words stepped on my words.

TATATA. *(Frosty.)* Well, I'll just go eat horse dung and die!

ARG. Okay, let's try it again. Ready? And … action!

UG. *("Acting.")* It is many rains and white seasons ago. The tribe is very hungry and I am seeking boar with my very best sharp stick. I wade through a silent, white blanket of freshly fallen snow.

ARG. Stop! What's with this "waded my way and white blanket?"

UG. I added new words. This play is a work in progress, you know. It's not written in stone.

IG. *(Indicates flat rock.)* Actually, it is written in stone. I have it right here.

UG. You know what I mean!

TATATA. Well, thanks for telling us!

UG. This is my play. I can do whatever I like with it!

ARG. It's not "your" play! It's *our* play!

TATATA. Yeah! We're all putting our asses on the line here for this!

BANDALA. Stop picking on Ug!

TATATA. You're just pissed he's with me now!

BANDALA. Bite me!

TATATA. Sorry! I'm tryin' to cut down on hair! *(Tatata and Bandala lunge for each other.)*

BANDALA. Bitch!

TATATA. Fat ass! *(Arg breaks up the squabble.)*

ARG. Ladies! Ladies!

BANDALA. Your boar sucks!

TATATA. What was that, "costume girl"?

ARG. Ladies! Could we *please* stop this arguing and practice the play?

TATATA. Don't look at me! *I'm* not the one holding things up!

ARG. Fine, people take your places. And let's go all the way through this time without stopping to argue or throw stones.

TATATA. Yeah, c'mon. *The Boar and Ug* opens tomorrow night.

BOB. Hold it. Wait. The title of this play is *Ug and the Boar*, not *The Boar and Ug*.

TATATA. I know, but you wanna know the truth? It's flat. You're Ug, you look for a boar, you call it *Ug and the Boar*. You hear that title and there's no surprise.

IG. It surprises *me*.

ARG. Me, too.

BOB. I'm surprised every time I hear it.

TATATA. But there's no bend. No hook. *The Boar and Ug* … that says it all.

BOB. Does this change in titles affect the costumes at all?

TATATA. No.

BOB. Good.

TATATA. And Ug … some of the words in your play … No offense, but I think they need to be changed.

UG. *(Shocked.)* Change? My words?!?

TATATA. Just a few of them.

UG. I don't want you to think I'm saying this just because I wrote this play but …

TATATA. But what?

UG. I think my play is absolutely perfect.

TATATA. It is perfect. It's just that a few of the words, well … we've heard them before.

UG. *(Explodes.)* This is the first play ever! No one's ever heard anything before!

TATATA. *(Wounded kitten.)* I'm just trying to help a little. If I'm not allowed to make a teensy-weensy suggestion …

UG. No, you are. You're allowed.

BANDALA. *(Sotto.)* Oh, brother!

TATATA. *(Sexily.)* Don't you want your play to be the best it can be?

UG. Well, I uh …

TATATA. It just needs a few iddy biddy changes. You'll see. Let's find a rock and make some notes.

UG. *(Lost in her eyes.)* 'kay … *(Tatata leads Ug to a corner of the cave where they chat silently. Tatata is able to manipulate whatever she wants from Ug. Bandala and Arg watch them as their hearts break. Music up.)*

SONG: AS IF I CARE

BANDALA.
LOVE JUST CAME AND WENT
AS IF I CARE
THEY LOOK SO CONTENT
AS IF I CARE
I KNOW EVERYTHING THEY'RE FEELING,
THE CLOSENESS THAT THEY SHARE
ONCE MY HEART WAS REELING
NOW IT'S NUMB
AS IF I CARE

ARG. MAN, THAT GIRL IS HOT
AS IF I CARE
THOUGHT I HAD A SHOT
AS IF I CARE
WE COULD HAVE HAD A ROMANCE
AN HONEST ONE IS RARE

THOUGHT I HAD A CHANCE
BUT SHE'S WITH HIM
AS IF I CARE
BANDALA and ARG.
   FINDING MY WAY IN A WINDING MAZE
   I DOUBT THAT I WILL EVER BE THE SAME
   WISHING IS MEANINGLESS NOWADAYS
   COULD BE I ONLY HAVE MYSELF TO BLAME
BANDALA.
   DREAMING WAS A JOKE
   AS IF I CARE
ARG.
   DISAPPEARED IN SMOKE
   AS IF I CARE
BANDALA.
   MY FUTURE'S IN THE PAST
   AS IF I CARE
ARG.
   IT CAME AND WENT SO FAST
   AS IF I CARE
BANDALA and ARG.
   IT'S NO USE TO KEEP PRETENDING
   I HAVEN'T GOT A PRAYER
   THERE'S NO HAPPY ENDING
   NOT FOR ME
   AS IF I CARE

   YOU'D WHISPER MY NAME AND MY HEART WOULD MELT
   NO ONE ELSE COULD MAKE ME FEEL THAT WAY
   I'D ALWAYS HOPED THAT'S THE WAY YOU FELT
   BUT YOU'RE IN SOMEONE ELSE'S ARMS TODAY
ARG.
   I BET HE'S TELLING LIES
   AS IF I CARE
BANDALA.
   SHE'S STARING IN HIS EYES
   AS IF I CARE
ARG.
   SHADOWS CROSS MY MIND

AS IF I CARE
BANDALA.
   AND NOW I'M LEFT BEHIND
   AS IF I CARE
ARG.
   USED TO KNOW WHERE I WAS GOING
BANDALA.
   THOUGHT THAT LIFE WAS FAIR
BANDALA and ARG.
   I'M BETTER OFF NOT KNOWING HOW THIS ENDS
   AS IF I CARE
   THERE'S NOTHING TO BELIEVE IN ANY MORE!
ARG.
   AS IF I CARE!

(Song ends. Ug and Tatata return from their conference and the others gather around. Tatata carries a flat rock with writing on it.)

TATATA. Okay, everybody we made a few changes and now the play is even better. Take a look. See what we've got. This is what we're going with.

ARG. You changed the title of the play?

IG. Again?

TATATA. I know, we went back and forth on that so many times. *Ug and the Boar, The Boar and Ug* …

IG. So what's the title now?

BOB. As if we have to ask!

TATATA. We cut away all the fat and now the title is just … *Boar!* Like it?

ARG. No.

BANDALA. Hate it.

IG. That sucks.

BOB. Utter crap.

TATATA. It's great. Trust me. It'll grow on you. Arg, this area where we do the play … It needs to be, I don't know … bigger somehow.

ARG. *(Exasperated.)* This is a *cave!* You can't make it any bigger!

TATATA. Well, do what you can. Maybe move some rocks around or something. And my hair, I'm going to change that. It's got to flow. Not flick. But flow. All flowy and, you know, flowy! Ooo! I need a new costume!

BOB. *(Exasperated.)* What happened to this one!

TATATA. I don't like it anymore.

BOB. *(Breaking down.)* This is your third costume today! I can't stand this! This is insane! I can't take the pressure!!! *(Bob throws down the costume he's been work-*

ing on and storms off to a corner, where he weeps.)

TATATA. He'll be okay. I don't like my choice of fur. I'm thinking … lion! Yes, lion fur would be perfect!

BANDALA. But you're playing a boar. Why would you use lion fur?

TATATA. You don't get it?

BANDALA. Not at all.

TATATA. That's why you'll always be you — and I'll be a star. *(Tatata exits as Bandala reacts angrily.)*

BANDALA. I'll kill her! *(Bandala exits after Tatata.)*

ARG. No, don't! *(Arg exits after Bandala.)*

IG. Hey, Ug … If you wrote a play about something that happened in more than one day …

UG. Uh-huh.

IG. How would you show going from one day to the next?

UG. Easy. I'd cover the fire with a wet skin … *(Ug covers the fire with a skin. The lights slowly fade out.)* Then I'd make it light again. *(The skin is lifted off the fire by Ig. He's in the midst of making dinner. Ug and the others are busy making their cave ready for their upcoming evening with the Tall People. Tatata does little to help.)*

ARG. Ig, how's dinner coming?

IG. The wolf? It's almost done.

UG. Is it tough and grisly?

IG. Yup.

UG. *(Relieved.)* Good. Oolooki loves his wolf tough and grisly. Okay, now remember everyone … when the Tall People get here just act natural.

ARG. Right.

IG. Gotcha.

BANDALA. Natural.

BOB. It's a good mislead.

UG. We don't want to mention the play until *after* dinner.

IG. Not a word.

BANDALA. We'll bring it up casually.

BOB. An off-handed remark.

ARG. Just in passing.

TATATA. No big deal.

UG. It's a little something the tribe thought up.

ARG. It's not like we *have* to show it to them.

BANDALA. Let them ask.

TATATA. Let them beg.

IG. *(Mocking.)* "Please let us see this thing you call a play!" Ha ha!

ARG. Well, I guess everything is all set.

BOB. *(To Ig.)* You make a dip?

IG. Yup.

BANDALA. There's nothing left to do.

UG. There is one thing we can do. We can speak to the Big Powerful Man or Woman or Wolf or Buffalo who lives in the sky and ask for help. The reputation of this tribe is at stake tonight. This night will decide what the rest of our lives will be like. Whether we live in honor or in shame. I think we should join together in a humble act of prayer. *(They all bow their heads and the moment becomes very solemn. Music up.)*

SONG: NOW YOU OWE ME

UG.

I'VE THROWN MY LIFE, INTO THIS PLAY
GAVE MY GIRL … GAVE MY HEART … GAVE MY SOUL
GAVE EVERYTHING AWAY

NOW YOU OWE ME, YES YOU DO
OWE ME BIG (YES YOU DO)
YES YOU DO (YES YOU DO)
YES YOU DO (OH YES OH YES OH YES YOU DO)

GAVE UP MY HEALTH, HAD SLEEPLESS NIGHTS
AND MY DIRECTOR! MY DESIGNER! AND MY ACTORS!
DON'T ASK ABOUT THE FIGHTS!

NOW YOU OWE ME, YES YOU DO
OWE ME BIG (YES YOU DO)
YES YOU DO (YES YOU DO)
YES YOU DO (OH YES OH YES OH YES YOU DO)

YOU OWE ME GLORY, YOU OWE ME FAME
I WON'T BE A MARTYR, I WON'T BE A PAIN
I'VE BEEN A GOOD BOY, DEVOTED THROUGH AND THROUGH
HOW ABOUT A LITTLE BREAK HERE
JUST TELL ME WHAT TO DO

(Trombone solo.)

I'D PRAY TO THE MOON, TO THE STARS IN SPACE
I'D PRAY TO THIS ROCK, IF THAT WOULD HELP MY CASE
I HUMBLY ASK, IN A REVERENT VOICE
(Spoken.) "Please let this play of mine become a 'Critic's Choice.'"
MY REPUTATION IS ON THE LINE
NO TIME TO BEG ... NO TIME TO PLEAD ... NO TIME TO GROVEL
AND THERE'S NO TIME TO WHINE
I THINK YOU OWE ME, OH YES YOU DO
OWE ME BIG (YES YOU DO)
YES YOU DO (YES YOU DO)
YES YOU DO (OH YES OH YES OH YES YOU DO)

I THINK YOU OWE ME, YES YOU DO
OWE ME BIG (YES YOU DO)
YES YOU DO (YES YOU DO)
YES YOU DO (OH YES OH YES OH YES YOU DO)
YES YOU DO (YES YOU DO)
YES YOU DO (YES YOU DO)
YES YOU DO! (OH YES OH YES OH YES YOU DO, OH YES OH YES
OH YES YOU DO OH YES OH YES OH YES YOU DO)
(Song ends.)
IG. I always feel so good right after we pray. *(Arg looks outside and reacts excitedly.)*
ARG. They're coming! They're coming! The Tall People are coming!
UG. So soon?
IG. They made good time.
BOB. You know the Tall People. They take big steps.
UG. Remember, everyone ... we don't mention the play until *after* dinner!
BANDALA. After.
UG. Not before.
TATATA. Got it.
UG. It's no big thing. It's just a little something we ...
UG. Shhh! Shhh! It's them! It's them! *(Fatalataba enters.)*
FATALATABA. *(Stately and ceremonious.)* Greetings! I am Fatalataba! I am chief envoy, main friend, suck-up, confidant, cohort, secretary, right-hand man, deputy, fall guy, parasitic hanger-on, and advisor to Chief Oolooki! *(Then.)* Hi, Bob.
BOB. Hey, guy. *(Bob and Fatalataba exchange smiles.)*
FATALATABA. Get ready to meet and greet Chief Oolooki. The high, exalted, grand eminent, sublime and so fine, numero uno, tip-top wizard, pace setting, whiz-bang, master and leader of the Tall People. A man whose power and author-

ity reaches all the way from the deep canyon from which there is no return to the lake with salty tasting water! Get ready to meet and greet the most incredible, most fantastic, bombastic leader I've ever known! A man known all over the world for his wisdom, compassion, good looks, and smarts. The only man in the world who can do the grunt-naked-nah-nah-big-tickle and eat dinner at the same time. The man who once saved my life simply by saying "Schmuck, look out for the cliff!" *(Music up.)* A totally awesome individual whose record against lions is fifteen and oh with one draw. He is the undisputed Duke of Danger, the King with Zing, the Flirt Who Can Hurt, the Master of Disaster, the Count of Monte Fist-o! Let's get ready to be humble! Here is the one, the only … Chief Ooooooooolooooooki!!! *(Chief Oolooki enters.)*

SONG: KING NEANDERTHAL

OOLOOKI.
 I'M SO POWERFUL I'M SOMEONE YOU SHOULD FEAR
FATALATABA. But he's fair. He's not ruthless.
OOLOOKI.
 HANDSOME TOO I WISH THEY'D INVENT THE MIRROR
FATALATABA. Our research group is working on that.
OOLOOKI.
 I'VE BEEN AN ICON SINCE I INVENTED FIRE
FATALATABA. No one knows how he does it.
OOLOOKI.
 I'M THE OBJECT OF ALL ENVY AND DESIRE
FATALATABA. I adore him and I'm straight.
OOLOOKI.
 IF WE HAD TROPHIES THEY WOULD ALL BE MINE
FATALATABA. He'd like to thank all the little people.
OOLOOKI.
 ONE DAY THEY'RE GONNA MAKE MY CAVE A SHRINE
FATALATABA. We'd call it "Oolooki Land."
OOLOOKI.
 EVEN THOUGH
 I DON'T BRAG
 BEING HUMBLE'S SUCH A DRAG
 WHEN YOU KNOW
 THAT YOU'RE KING NEANDERTHAL

I'M THE KING NEANDERTHAL
SOME MAY GROVEL, SOME MAY CRAWL
BUT NOT KING NEANDERTHAL
I'M THE SLICKEST OF THEM ALL
I'M THE BRAVEST GUY — I'M KING NEANDERTHAL

I BANISH PEOPLE STARING AT MY THRONE
FATALATABA. Change of leadership is stressful.
OOLOOKI.
AND I KEEP A LIST OF WOMEN THAT I'VE KNOWN
FATALATABA. It's a long list. I've seen it.
OOLOOKI.
ALL THE CHILDREN IN OUR TRIBE WERE MADE BY ME
FATALATABA. Handsome kids. And well behaved!
OOLOOKI.
NO ONE ELSE CAN MATE, THAT WAS MY DECREE
FATALATABA. You don't miss it after a while.
OOLOOKI.
OTHERS PRAISE AND HONOR ME, OF COURSE
FATALATABA. What's not to praise?
OOLOOKI.
AND THAT'S THE WAY IT SHOULD BE WHEN YOU'RE BOSS
FATALATABA. He's got tenure, you know.
OOLOOKI.
I'M THE MAN
OF THE HOUR
I'M ASTONISHED AT MY POWER
'CAUSE YOU KNOW
I'M KING NEANDERTHAL

I'M THE KING NEANDERTHAL
MAMA THINKS THAT I'M A DOLL
I'M HER KING NEANDERTHAL
GOTTA GIVE MY MOM A CALL

I'M A THOUGHTFUL SON — I'M KING NEANDERTHAL
(Dance instrumental.)

I'M THE KING NEANDERTHAL

I'M THE TALLEST OF THE TALL
I'M THE KING NEANDERTHAL
I CAN DAZZLE AND ENTHRALL
I'M THE HIPPEST GUY — I'M KING NEANDERTHAL

I'M COOL AND I RULE — I'M KING NEANDERTHAL
(Song ends. Oolooki extends his hand and wiggles his fingers until Ug and his tribe can't help but notice every one of his fingers has a ring on it.) Thank you. You're beautiful. Thank you. Thank you, ladies and gentlemen. You're too kind. Thank you.
UG. What are those?
OOLOOKI. *(Playing dumb.)* What are what?
ARG. Those things.
BANDALA. On your fingers.
TATATA. They're very pretty.
OOLOOKI. Oh these? These pretty things that ring the fingers on my hands?
UG. Yes.
FATALATABA. It's something new and trendy. Chief Oolooki invented it all by himself!
OOLOOKI. As you can see, I invented these things that ring my fingers.
BOB. What do you call these things that ring your fingers?
OOLOOKI. I call these things that ring my fingers … finger thingies! *(Everyone else "ooos" and "ahhhs.")*
TATATA. Catchy name.
IG. Way cool.
BOB. It's a little obvious …
OOLOOKI. I came up with the concept. The women in my tribe did the actual work.
FATALATABA. And they were glad to do it for him.
OOLOOKI. I said, "Make me one for each finger." They made all nine. I can't be bothered with actual labor. I'm an idea man.
FATALATABA. He is. He has ideas he hasn't even thought of yet!
BANDALA. I predict that finger thingies will catch on quickly.
ARG. Everyone will be wearing finger thingies and soon.
FATALATABA. Everyone except Chief Oolooki. By then he will have moved on to something entirely new.
OOLOOKI. I set trends, others follow.
UG. Well, we're glad you got here.
ARG. Safe and sound.
TATATA. In one piece.

BANDALA. Sometimes you invite people for the next full moon …

TATATA. They have no idea when the next full moon is.

BOB. It makes meal planning impossible.

UG. They guess wrong, they show up a day early.

ARG. A day late.

BANDALA. Or not at all!

OOLOOKI. We never miss a full moon. Now that we have a … *(Fatalataba unfolds an animal skin to reveal a crude but workable calendar. Ug and his tribe are amazed.)* Calendar!

OTHERS. Gasp!

IG. Wow!

BANDALA. Goodness!

TATATA. Holy!

ARG. Mama!

BOB. Gracious!

UG. A calendar! You have a calendar! Wow, a calendar! Look, it's a calendar! An actual calendar! What's a calendar?

FATALATABA. It's a chart that keeps track of all the days of the year.

OOLOOKI. *(Annoyed.)* I wanted to tell them!

FATALATABA. Sorry.

OOLOOKI. It's a chart that keeps track of all the days of the year. All two hundred of them.

FATALATABA. Another push into the future, courtesy of Chief Oolooki.

OOLOOKI. I figured it out in my head. Our women did the actual work.

FATALATABA. And they were glad to do it for us. *(Ug and his tribe examine the calendar more closely.)*

UG. Wow.

BOB. Weird.

IG. Freaky.

UG. These marks are the days?

OOLOOKI. Yeeee-up.

ARG. And these marks are the seasons?

OOLOOKI. You got it.

TATATA. What's this at the top of your calendar?

OOLOOKI. It's a picture. Three puppies in a basket. People seem to like it. *(Then.)* Say, is that wolf I smell cooking?

IG. You betcha.

ARG. It's been a long time since we've had wolf.

UG. Many moons.

BANDALA. Many many.

TATATA. Forever.

FATALATABA. We have it all the time.

UG. *(Quick to cover.)* So do we.

ARG. Had it yesterday.

BANDALA. I'm sick of wolf.

IG. I think you'll like this wolf. I'm also cooking a snake appetizer.

OOLOOKI. You let a *child* prepare your meals?

UG. Sure.

BOB. I've been laying back. Taking some "me" time.

TATATA. Besides, Ig is a good cook.

ARG. He always follows the recipe.

UG. And he never falls in the fire. At least not yet. *(Music up.)*

OOLOOKI. But cooking wolf is complicated.

FATALATABA. Extremely complicated.

IG. Aw, cooking wolf is easy!

SONG: COOKING SONG (REPRISE)

IG.
> WOLVES LIVE ALL ALONE
> OR WOLVES LIVE IN A FLOCK
> IF YOU WANT YOURSELF A FRESH WOLF
> YOU GET YOURSELF A ROCK
>
> THEN YOU TAKE THE ROCK
> AND HIT HIM ON THE HEAD
> WHEN HE GETS A SLEEPY LOOK
> YOU'LL KNOW THAT HE IS DEAD

FATALATABA. We don't use a rock. We use a club.

IG.
> THEN YOU GATHER SOME WOOD
> AND THROW HIM IN THE FIRE
> YOU CAN ADD SOME DIRT FOR FLAVORING
> WHATEVER YOU DESIRE
>
> COOK HIM FOR HALF A DAY
> POKE HIM WITH A STICK
> SERVE IT WHILE IT'S PIPING HOT

YOU KNOW YOU'VE DONE THE TRICK!

FOR A BOY
ON A GROWING SPURT
A NICE LITTLE SNACK
OF RHINO OR YAK
WHAT COULD IT HURT?

YOU'LL CRY
TO SEE AN ANIMAL DIE
BUT THAT WILL SOON PASS
ALONG WITH THE GAS
LEAVE ROOM FOR THE PIE

ALL.
   SABRE TOOTH PIE!

OOLOOKI. That's all well and good, but you can't cook an appetizer with the main meal.

FATALATABA. It's impossible.

OOLOOKI. Can't be done.

IG. Sure it can.
   SNAKES LIVE ALL ALONE
   OR SNAKES LIVE IN A FLOCK
   IF YOU WANT YOURSELF A FRESH SNAKE
   YOU GET YOURSELF A ROCK

   THEN YOU TAKE THE ROCK
   AND HIT HIM ON THE HEAD
   WHEN HE GETS A SLEEPY LOOK
   YOU'LL KNOW THAT HE IS DEAD

OOLOOKI. I hope you're not serving that deadly red snake. You know, "the Snake You Take One Bite of and It Makes You Dead."

IG. No!

FATALATABA. How would you know?

IG. 'Cause I already took a bite!

OOLOOKI. Yeah?

IG. I'm not dead!

ALL. Ahh!

IG.
   THEN YOU GATHER SOME WOOD

AND THROW HIM IN THE FIRE
YOU CAN ADD SOME DIRT FOR FLAVORING
WHATEVER YOU DESIRE

COOK HIM FOR HALF A DAY
POKE HIM WITH A STICK
SERVE IT WHILE IT'S PIPING HOT
YOU KNOW YOU'VE DONE THE TRICK!

(Spoken.) Don't eat a snake sideways! You'll choke.

ALL.
YOU KNOW YOU'VE DONE THE TRICK!

(Song ends.)

IG. It'll be ready soon. After you throw away the black, crusty part you'll find good wolf meat underneath.

OOLOOKI. *(Disappointed.)* Oh, I see. Well, yes. I'm sure.

UG. Something wrong?

OOLOOKI. No, not really.

BOB. What is it?

OOLOOKI. Nothing.

BOB. Don't try and kid us. Something's wrong. Spit it out.

OOLOOKI. Well, it's just that when we eat wolf …

FATALATABA. And we eat wolf all the time!

OOLOOKI. We don't *have* a black, crusty part.

UG. You don't?

OOLOOKI. We put our wolf on a stick and place it *above* the fire. Then our women slowly turn the wolf.

FATALATABA. And they're glad to do it for us!

OOLOOKI. The wolf cooks slower. There's never a black, crusty part.

IG. *(Hurt.)* Oh.

OOLOOKI. Aw, what the heck! It's been a long time since we ate wolf the "old fashioned" way.

FATALATABA. Yeah, it'll remind us of the wolf our *grandmothers* used to make.

OOLOOKI. Way back when!

FATALATABA. "Way back when!"

OOLOOKI. In "olden days"!

FATALATABA. "Olden days"! You're killin' me! *(Oolooki and Fatalataba roll with laughter. Ug has had enough.)*

UG. *(Blurts.)* We have a play!

OOLOOKI. A what?

UG. A play! We have one!

OOLOOKI. And what, may I ask, is a "play"?

UG. It's a new way of telling stories. It's something we made up. All by ourselves.

BANDALA. No one else has it.

IG. No other tribe.

TATATA. Just us.

ARG. It's new.

BOB. And it's trendy.

ARG. It's an artistic expression.

UG. It reenacts a moment in the tribe's history.

TATATA. The tribe's *proud* history.

BANDALA. It speaks of our bravery and honor.

IG. Our courage.

BOB. Our pluck.

OOLOOKI. Oh, our tribe celebrates our triumphs as well!

FATALATABA. Too many to mention!

OOLOOKI. We speak of them often.

FATALATABA. Every night!

OOLOOKI. The men sing and the women make drum sounds.

FATALATABA. And they're glad to do it for us. *(Oolooki and Fatalataba break out into a ditty.)*

OOLOOKI and FATALATABA. *(Sing together.)*
  GULAH FOUND A FISH
  GULAH FOUND A FISH
  GULAH FOUND A FISH
  AND THEN WE ATE IT!

(Ug and his tribe look at Oolooki and Fatalataba then break out laughing.)

OOLOOKI. What! What!

BOB. This isn't some stupid ass song!

ARG. That you just sing!

TATATA. Or some story!

BANDALA. That you just tell!

UG. This is a play! We reenact the entire incident as though you were there. *(Oolooki and Fatalataba gasp.)*

OOLOOKI. No!

FATALATABA. Impossible!

UG. I pretend to be myself long, long ago.

IG. Tatata pretends to be a boar.

TATATA. Long, long ago.

UG. The setting from long ago is these three walls.

OOLOOKI. And where am I during all this?

ARG. You sit behind the fourth wall.

OOLOOKI. But I see no wall!

BOB. That's because it's not there. Work with us!

OOLOOKI. How can there be a fourth wall if it's not there?

UG. Because we *pretend* it's there.

OOLOOKI. Ah! And I pretend it's there, too?

BANDALA. No!

UG. If you did that you couldn't see the play!

ARG. We're actors. We totally ignore you …

BANDALA. As we desperately seek your approval.

OOLOOKI. And you call this a play?

UG. Yes.

OOLOOKI. A thing where you are you, but not you now, you then. *(Re Tatata.)* And she, she is not herself at all. She is an animal. But not an animal now, an animal then. And none of you are here, you're somewhere else. And I pretend to be there with you as I sit behind a wall that you can see but I can't.

UG. Exactly!

BOB. I never heard it explained better.

OOLOOKI. *(Calm.)* Well, thank you. Yes. *(Explodes.)* I don't even know what I *said! (Then.)* This sounds like dark sorcery to me!

BANDALA. Typical!

ARG. The thinking of a small mind!

UG. If something is too artsy to grasp, you dismiss it as … *(Mocking.)* "dark magic."

IG. This is not sorcery!

BOB. This is theater!

TATATA. And it's real artsy!

BOB. Way beyond what you're used to!

OOLOOKI. Impossible!

BOB. If you grasp half of it, it'll be a freakin' miracle!

OOLOOKI. I should like to see this thing you call a play.

UG. Then you will.

OOLOOKI. What shall I do?

ARG. Sit here and face the fire.

FATALATABA. Me, too?

UG. *(Patronizing.)* Would you like to see the play?

FATALATABA. Yes, very much.

UG. Then sit and face the fire.

FATALATABA. What else do we do?

BANDALA. Nothing.

BOB. That's the great thing about seeing a play. Once you get there, all you have to do is sit on your ass.

OOLOOKI. I can do that!

FATALATABA. Me, too!

UG. Just lay back.

ARG. Relax.

BANDALA. Bring no expectations.

TATATA. Let the play think for you.

OOLOOKI. I'm frightened. *(Ug puts a friendly hand on Oolooki's shoulder.)*

UG. We were, too, the first time. It'll be okay. *(Ug and his tribe begin to exit.)*

FATALATABA. *(Alarmed.)* They're leaving!

OOLOOKI. Where are you going?

UG. *(Exasperated.)* We're going out … so we can come back in.

OOLOOKI. Oh.

UG. The next time you see us … it will be in the play.

OOLOOKI.	FATALATABA.
Ah!	Aha! Gotcha!

(Ug and his tribe have almost exited. Fatalataba reaches into his pouch and takes out something in a dried leaf. As he opens the leaf it makes a great deal of noise.)

UG. What's that?

FATALATABA. Hmm?

UG. What is that noise?

FATALATABA. Oh, on the journey here I found some sweet-juicy-red-things-that-won't-make-you-dead. I wrapped them in this leaf.

UG. And you're eating them?

FATALATABA. Well …

UG. Now?

FATALATABA. I … uh …

UG. During my play!

FATALATABA. Uh …

UG. Did you ever stop to think maybe the other people in the audience came to hear my play? Not to listen to the sound of you having dinner? You *tourist!* *(Fatalataba puts his sweets away as Ug and his tribe exit. Oolooki and Fatalataba are alone now. They sit in silence for several beats.)*

FATALATABA. *(Sotto to Oolooki.)* Boy, he was mad.

OOLOOKI. *(Shrugs it off.)* Writers.

FATALATABA. Yeah. *(They sit in silence for a few more beats.)*

OOLOOKI. You know what I'm thinking?

FATALATABA. What's that?

OOLOOKI. We head back home right after dinner.

FATALATABA. How come?

OOLOOKI. We leave any later we'll hit traffic.

FATALATABA. Aha. (*They sit in silence for a few more beats.*)

OOLOOKI. I wonder what we do now?

FATALATABA. Just sit here, I guess.

OOLOOKI. You know what I'm hoping?

FATALATABA. What's that?

UG. (*Offstage.*) Shut up!

OOLOOKI. Sorry. (*Ug's play begins. Arg, Bob and Ig enter carrying drums as they slowly beat in the background. A beat, then Ug enters carrying a sharp stick.*)

UG. It is many rains and white seasons ago. The tribe is very hungry.

OOLOOKI. "Is?"

FATALATABA. He's using the present tense?

OOLOOKI. Shh!

UG. I am seeking boar with my very best sharp stick. I am weak and tired, near death from hunger. I stand little chance of winning a battle with a wild, ferocious boar.

OOLOOKI. (*Worried.*) Oh, my ...

FATALATABA. This is wonderful.

UG. My tribe is hungry! They are counting on me to bring home food! If I fail, they will all die.

OOLOOKI. This once happened to me!

FATALATABA. Me, too. I can relate totally!

UG. Seek boar, seek boar, seek boar, where is boar. I see no boar. Go home? Without food? No!

OOLOOKI. It's like I'm there with him.

FATALATABA. I know. I know.

UG. The cold, the dark, the wind ... I shiver with pain and hunger. I will not quit. I will not stop. I am brave and courageous, determined to become a hero!

OOLOOKI. He's so much like *me!*

FATALATABA. I was just going to say.

UG. Seek boar! Seek boar! Seek boar! Suddenly, look out, oh no, good golly, it's a wild, ferocious boar! (*Tatata enters dressed as the boar. Her boar costume is now a skimpy, fur bikini. Bandala, Arg, Bob, Ig, and Ug all serve as backup singers and chorus dancers for her. Music up.*)

SONG: I'M A BOAR

TATATA.
    I'M A BOAR
    I'M BUXOM AND BRAWNY
    FOR SURE
    WHAT'S MORE, I'M KNOWN IN FOLKLORE
    THERE'S SO MUCH IN STORE FOR THIS BOAR!

    I'M A PIG
    I'M BIG WHERE IT COUNTS
    YOU DIG?
    I'VE GOT A GREAT THINGAMAJIG
    THERE'S QUITE A RIG ON THIS PIG!

(Bridge.)
    THE TAIL IS SO SQUIGGLY
    ON THIS LITTLE PIGGLY
    I'LL LEAVE YOU FEELING AGOG
    I ROLL IN THE MUD
    COME AND JOIN ME YOU STUD
    I'LL BE YOUR PERSONAL HOG (OINK)
(The song kicks into high gear and has all the earmarks of a Las Vegas production number. Bandala will exit the cave unseen toward the end of this song.)
ALL.
    SHE'S A BOAR (I'M A BOAR)
    SHE'S BUXOM AND BRAWNY
    FOR SURE (WHADDYA THINK?)
    WHAT'S MORE, SHE'S KNOWN IN FOLKLORE (WAY BACK WHEN)
    THERE'S SO MUCH IN STORE FOR THIS BOAR! (2-3-4-5-6-7-8)

    SHE'S A PIG (I'M A PIG)
    SHE'S BIG WHERE IT COUNTS
    YOU DIG? (I GOTCHA)
    SHE'S GOT A GREAT — THINGAMAJIG (YES, I DO)
    THERE'S QUITE A RIG ON THIS PIG! (2-3-4-5-6-7-8)

(Bridge.)
    THE TAIL IS SO SQUIGGLY

ON THIS LITTLE PIGGLY
IT'LL LEAVE YOU FEELING AGOG
SHE'LL ROLL IN THE MUD
COME JOIN HER YOU STUD
SHE'LL BE YOUR PERSONAL HOG (OINK)

SHE'S A BOAR (I'M A BOAR)
AND WHEN SHE GETS ANGRY
SHE'LL ROAR (AHHH!!!)
HER ROAR HITS YOU RIGHT IN YOUR CORE
    (THAT'S YOUR MIDDLE)
THERE'S NO CHORE TO LOVIN' THIS BOAR! (2-3-4-5-6-7-8)

SHE'S NO GRUMP (NOT AT ALL)
GOT A SMILE TO MAKE YOUR HEART THUMP (BOOM BOOM)
AND A RUMP THAT'S SHAPELY AND PLUMP (HAVE A PINCH)
IT'S APPARENT — SHE ISN'T A FRUMP
TATATA.
    I SNORT AND I GROWL
    I GRUMBLE AND HOWL
    FOLKS HAVE BEEN KNOWN TO SAY WOW
    I ADMIRE MY TUSK
    FROM DAWN UNTIL DUSK
    THERE AIN'T NO FORGETTIN' THIS SOW
ALL.
    SHE'S A SWINE (I'M A SWINE)
    WHO'S MISUNDERSTOOD AND MALIGNED (BOO HOO)
    EVEN THOUGH SHE IS
    REALLY BENIGN (WHAT'S THAT MEAN?)
    AND PRETTY DARN CUTE FOR A SWINE

    SHE'S A BOAR (I'M A BOAR!)
    SHE'S A BOAR (I'M A BOAR!)
    SHE'S A BOAR!!!

(Song ends. Ug, Arg, Bob and Ig all strike chorus dancer poses around Tatata and hold them. Oolooki and Fatalataba are speechless. They look at each other, then look at Ug and his tribe again. After several long beats.)
OOLOOKI. That was …
UG. Yes?

OOLOOKI. That was …

UG. It was what? (*Suddenly, Bandala bursts into the cave wearing the boar skin she wore in Act One. Bandala is especially fierce and frightening.*)

BANDALA. (*Roars.*) Aaarrrggg!!! Aaarrrggg!!! Aaarrrggg!!! Aaarrrggg!!! (*Bandala runs up to Oolooki and Fatalataba and growls in their faces. Fatalataba jumps into Oolooki's arms and stays there for a few beats. Ug understands what Bandala is up to and improvises.*)

UG. Wait! Here is *another* boar! This one is wild and ferocious! I shall fight this boar!

OOLOOKI. Don't!

FATALATABA. You'll die!

OOLOOKI. This boar is cranky!

TATATA. What is she *doing!*

UG. Ug is not afraid! Ug does not run! Ug fights the boar with his very best sharp stick! (*Ug and Bandala engage in a battle. They each spin, twirl and make a number of nice moves.*)

TATATA. She's ruining my play! (*Tatata crosses to a corner where she sulks.*)

BANDALA. (*Roars.*) Aaarrrggg!!! Aaarrrggg!!! Aaarrrggg!!!

OOLOOKI. Run!

FATALATABA. Get out of there, Ug!

UG. Ug is trying to kill the boar but Ug is pushed against a large stone! (*Ug and Bandala reenact this.*)

OOLOOKI. Look out, Ug!

FATALATABA. Save yourself!

UG. Ug fights the boar!

BANDALA. (*Growls.*) Aaarrrggg!!!

UG. The boar has very sharp teeth! Ug is cut! Ug is bleeding! Ug may die!

OOLOOKI. Don't die!

FATALATABA. Fight back!

BANDALA. (*Growls.*) Aaarrrggg!!! Aaarrrggg!!! (*Music up.*)

SONG: (TO GO) WHERE I'VE NEVER GONE BEFORE (REPRISE)

UG. Ug does not run! Ug is not afraid! Ug fights back with his very best sharp stick!

ALL.

   SUCH GENIUS AMONG US
   THE PRIDE THAT WE FEEL
   TO PLAY OUT A STORY
   AND MAKE IT SEEM REAL

THE PASSION, THE DRAMA
OF *UG AND THE BOAR*
IT'S TAKING US SOMEWHERE, SOMEWHERE
WE'VE NEVER BEEN BEFORE

(Ug pokes Bandala with his stick.)

UG. Ug fights! Ug is bleeding and weak, but Ug fights! Ug stabs the boar! Over and over! Take that, boar! Ug left his tribe behind! They are hungry!

OOLOOKI. He is so noble and brave!

FATALATABA. Just like you!

OOLOOKI. I know! I know!

UG. Ug stabs the boar over and over!

BANDALA. *(In "pain.")* Ew! Ew! Ew!

UG. Then comes a moment. Ug looks into the eyes of the boar and lets him see the picture of his own death soon to come. *(Ug takes Bandala into his arms in an embrace. The moment becomes gentle and romantic.)* Look, boar. Look into my eyes.

BANDALA. *(Sweetly.)* I see the land I will travel into. A land of all sunshine and no hunger.

UG. Give in to me and I shall put you there. *(Ug and Bandala share a long, romantic kiss. Oolooki and Fatalataba love it.)*

FATALATABA. Wow! Look what Ug is saying!

OOLOOKI. That the surrender of death can be as sweet and as gentle as the surrender of love.

FATALATABA. I thought he was saying it's fun to kiss a pig on the mouth.

(Oolooki smacks Fatlataba.)

OOLOOKI. Idiot! *(Note: These three parts are sung together.)*

BANDALA.

DAG-GERS ARE WHAT I GET
I'M LOOKED UPON BY OTHERS AS A THREAT
WHEN THEY HEAR … ME ROAR
I'LL SOAR … TO WHERE, I'VE NEVER GONE BEFORE

UG.	ARG.
SOMETHING AMAZING	AS TALENT SURROUNDS ME
IS HAPPENING TO ME	MY OPTIONS ASTOUND ME
THIS THING I AM DOING	MOVING PEOPLE AROUND ME
IT TRULY SETS ME FREE	TO GO … WHERE THEY HAVE
THE THRILL OF PERFORMING	NEVER GONE BEFORE
IS ONE I CAN'T IGNORE	
TO GO WHERE I'VE NEVER	
NEVER GONE BEFORE	

ALL.
  WHAT NEVER?
UG.
  NO NEVER
ALL.
  WHAT NEVER?
UG.
  NO, NOT EVER
ALL.
  WHERE WE'VE NEVER GONE BEFORE!
OLE!

(Song ends. Oolooki and Fatalataba applaud and whistle wildly.)

OOLOOKI. Yeah!

FATALATABA. Woo!

OOLOOKI. All right!

FATALATABA. Yeah!

OOLOOKI. Wonderful!

FATALATABA. Terrific!

OOLOOKI. Fabulous!

UG. You liked it?

OOLOOKI. *Loved* it!

FATALATABA. So lifelike!

OOLOOKI. So real!

FATALATABA. Authentic!

OOLOOKI. Credible!

FATALATABA. Gripping action!

OOLOOKI. Fast and furious pace!

FATALATABA. Eye-popping effects!

OOLOOKI. Good structure!

FATALATABA. Solid emotional base!

OOLOOKI. Two thumbs up! *(Oolooki and Fatalataba hold up their thumbs.)* Of course, when what's-her-name came out and sang that stupid song!

FATALATABA. Who cared!

OOLOOKI. Boring!

FATALATABA. But then …

OOLOOKI. The ending!

FATALATABA. It recovered nicely!

OOLOOKI. *(Re Tatata.)* Take out everything she did and you've got something.

UG. The next time you see my play …

OOLOOKI. Yeah?

UG. It will be without Tatata. *(Ug and Bandala exchange loving smiles.)*

TATATA. *(Frosty.)* Well! *(Tatata walks off in a huff.)*

ARG. Why don't we feast on our burned wolf meat?

IG. I made a snake appetizer.

OOLOOKI. Yes. It seems to fit. You watch this thing called a play, then talk about it as you eat burned meat. *(Then.)* And on our journey home we will stop to speak to other tribes. We will tell them what we saw here this night. Ug and his tribe have invented a new way of telling stories. And now that we've seen it … we can never go back. Fatalataba …

FATALATABA. Yes?

OOLOOKI. This is an important day in history. Mark it on our calendar. *(Fatalataba marks the calendar.)*

FATALATABA. Augtember the 99th! Done!

OOLOOKI. Ug, you've invented something that will outlive you for all time. You will bask forever in the light of greatness. Who you are, your spirit, your fire, can never die.

UG. Thanks but … I'm not so sure about that.

BANDALA. I am!

OTHERS.

Gasp!   Really?!?   How come?!?   What do you mean?!?

BANDALA. Inside me I carry Ug's child.

OTHERS. Gasp!

UG. Why didn't you tell me?

BANDALA. You were dating the blonde.

UG. Oh.

BANDALA. I will bear this child, and Ug and I will love and raise him well. *(Music up.)* And our child will have children of his own and on and on. This is the way we shall never die. We can never, ever fade from this life. *(Oolooki, Fatalataba, Arg, Ig, and Tatata cross to the fire. They begin eating wolf while they have animated yet silent conversation.)*

SONG: TINGLE (REPRISE)

BANDALA.
  I WAS AFRAID
  WHAT COULD I DO?
UG.
  MY PLACE HAS ALWAYS BEEN

ALONGSIDE OF YOU
LOVING YOU SO
RIGHT FROM THE START
BANDALA.
  YOU HAVE MY TRUST
  AND YOU HAVE MY HEART
UG and BANDALA.
  WE'LL ALWAYS RECALL
  THE FEELING THAT BEGAN IT ALL

  THE TINGLE, TINGLE, TINGLE
(Song ends. Arg crosses to a sulking and hurt Tatata.)
ARG. You okay?
TATATA. I dunno …
ARG. That was a tough break.
TATATA. Yeah, well … *(Forties melodrama.)* These are tough times.
ARG. Did I tell you?
TATATA. What?
ARG. I'm writing a play.
TATATA. *(Lights up.)* You are?
ARG. Yeah, it's a one-woman show about a cave girl going through a mid-life crisis as she searches for her birth mother and fights a horrid disease.
TATATA. When can I read it?
ARG. As soon as I learn how to write!
TATATA. Oh, Arg! *(Tatata throws her arms around Arg.)*
BANDALA. Ug, why don't we show your story to other tribes and charge them meat and fish to see it?
UG. What a great idea! Yes! Yes! That way we'll never have to work for a living! *(Music up.)*

SONG: INCREDIBLE TIMES (REPRISE)

UG.
  OUR LITTLE GEM
  JUST SLAUGHTERED THEM
  WE COULDN'T GET MUCH HOTTER
  THE PLAY'S THE THING …
  HEY, THAT HAS A NICE RING
  WE'LL BE REMEMBERED

FOR BEING CARING
EXPERIMENTAL AND EVEN DARING
ALL.
   THESE ARE INCREDIBLE TIMES
   ALL YOU HAVE TO DO IS OPEN YOUR MIND
   THEN LOOK AROUND AND YOU WILL FIND
   LIFE IS A WONDER 'CAUSE THESE ARE INCREDIBLE

   THESE ARE INCREDIBLE TIMES
   ALL YOU HAVE TO DO IS OPEN YOUR EYES
   AND SEE THAT EVERYTHING IS JUST FINE
   IT SEEMS LIKE HEAVEN
   IT SEEMS LIKE HEAVEN
   IT SEEMS LIKE HEAVEN
   'CAUSE THESE ARE INCREDIBLE TIMES

   INCREDIBLE TIMES!!!
(The lights fade to black. Lights up — curtain call. Music up.)

SONG: SOMETHING WE CALL A PLAY (REPRISE)

ALL.
   WHETHER SMASH OR DUD
   THEATRE GETS IN YOUR BLOOD
   AND YOU KNOW YOU'RE IN IT TO STAY NO OTHER ART
   GETS YOU HOOKED FROM THE START
   LETS YOU BE SOMEONE ELSE FOR A DAY
(Music stops.)
UG. Be careful of lions on your way home! *(Music resumes.)*
MEN.
   LIKE SOMETHING
   SOMETHING WE CALL A …
WOMEN.
   SOMETHING, SOMETHING WE CALL A …
ALL.
   SOMETHING WE CALL A PLAY!
(Song ends.)

THE END

PROPERTY LIST

Sharp stick
Wooden plates
Fur
Knife
Cooked boar
Drink cup, water
Bear skin
Tree bark
Fur bikini
Flat stones with writing
Costumes in progress
Animal skin
9 finger rings
Animal skin calendar
Pouch, dried leaf, red berries
Drums
Cooked wolf, cooked snake

SOUND EFFECTS

Thunk
Crunching of dried leaf
Drumbeats